THE COMPLETE GUIDE TO THE VIZSLA

Tarah Schwartz

LP Media Inc. Publishing

For information address LP Media Inc. Publishing, 3178 253rd Ave. NW, Isanti, MN 55040

www.lpmedia.org

Publication Data

Tarah Schwartz

The Complete Guide to the Vizsla - First edition.

Summary: "Successfully raising a Vizsla Dog from puppy to old age" - Provided by publisher.

ISBN: 978-1-954288-32-4

[1. Vizsla - Non-Fiction] I. Title.

This book has been written with the published intent to provide accurate and authoritative information in regard to the subject matter included. While every reasonable precaution has been taken in preparation of this book the author and publisher expressly disclaim responsibility for any errors, omissions, or adverse effects arising from the use or application of the information contained inside. The techniques and suggestions are to be used at the reader's discretion and are not to be considered a substitute for professional veterinary care. If you suspect a medical problem with your dog, consult your veterinarian.

Design by Sorin Rădulescu

First paperback edition, 2021

TABLE OF CONTENTS

CHAPTER 1

The History of the Vizsla 1
The Origins of the Vizsla 1
The Vizsla's Influence on Other Breeds 4
The Modern Vizsla 5

CHAPTER 2

The Vizsla 7
Physical Characteristics 7
Behavioral Characteristics 9
Vizslas as Family Dogs 10
Vizslas as Sport and Performance Dogs 12
Vizslas and Prey Drive 12
Is the Vizsla Right for You? 14

CHAPTER 3

Finding Your Ideal Vizsla 15
Purchasing from a Breeder vs. Adopting from a Rescue 15
Choosing a Reputable Breeder 19
Questions to Ask a Breeder Before Bringing a Vizsla Home . . . 22
Choosing a Reputable Rescue 23
Questions to Ask a Rescue Before Bringing a Vizsla Home 24
Contracts and Guarantees 26

Health Testing and Certifications 27

How to Choose Your Ideal Dog 29

CHAPTER 4

Preparing Your Family for a Vizsla 31

Yearly Costs of Owning a Vizsla 31

Preparing Children 36

Mutual Respect 38

Preparing Your Other Pets 38

Family Commitment 40

CHAPTER 5

Preparing Your Home for Your New Vizsla 41

Creating a Safe Area Indoors 41

Necessary Supplies 44

Crates and Crate Training 47

Dog-Proofing Your House 50

Indoor Dangers 50

Outdoor Dangers 53

CHAPTER 6

Bringing Your New Vizsla Home 55

Planning Your Vizsla's Arrival 55

Developing a Schedule 56

Picking Your Vizsla Up from the Breeder 56

Bringing Your Vizsla Home from the Rescue 58

The Ride Home 58

The First Night Home 61

CHAPTER 7

The First Few Weeks 65

Standing by Your Expectations 65

Establishing Household Rules 66

Puppy Problems 69

Adult Dog Problems 74

Leaving Your Dog Home Alone 75

Training Classes 76

Taking It Slow 77

CHAPTER 8

Health and Wellness

Health and Wellness 79

Choosing a Veterinarian 79

What to Expect During the First Visit 81

Tail Docking 83

Dangerous Foods 85

Common Health Problems in Vizslas 85

    Hip and Elbow Dysplasia 86

    Eye Problems 87

    Heart Problems 88

    Autoimmune Thyroiditis 88

    Sebaceous Adenitis 88

Vizslas and Extreme Temperatures 89

CHAPTER 9

Housetraining

Housetraining 91

Different Options for Housetraining 91

The First Few Weeks 93

The Importance of Consistency 95

Positive Reinforcement 95

Cleaning Up 97

Playpens and Doggy Doors 99

CHAPTER 10

Socialization

Socialization 101

The Importance of Good Socialization 101

Socializing Puppies 103

Socializing Adult Dogs 105

Lifelong Socialization 107

Dealing with High Prey Drives 107
Dealing with Fear 109

CHAPTER 11

The Multi-pet Household 111
Introducing a Puppy to Other Animals 111
Introducing an Adult Dog to Other Animals 114
Vizslas and Small Pets 114
Fighting and Bad Behavior 116
Raising Multiple Puppies from the Same Litter . . . 118
Options if Your Pets Don't Get Along 118

CHAPTER 12

Training your Vizsla 121
The Importance of Early Training 121
Operant Conditioning Basics 122
Essential Commands 125
    Name Recognition 125
    Sit 126
    Lie Down 128
    Stay 130
    Recall 130
    Drop It 132
    Leave It 132
Advanced Commands 133

CHAPTER 13

Nutrition 135
The Importance of a Balanced Diet 135
Basic Nutrition 137
    Proteins and Amino Acids 137
    Fat and Fatty Acids 139
    Carbohydrates 140
Feeding Puppies vs. Adult Dogs 140

Commercial Diets 142

Homemade Diets 143

Weight Management 146

Food Allergies and Intolerances 148

Performance and Sport Dog Nutrition 149

CHAPTER 14

Physical and Mental Exercise 151

The Importance of Physical Exercise 151

    Exercising Puppies 154

    Exercising Adult Dogs 154

The Importance of Mental Exercise 155

Dog Sports 159

    Pointing Breed Field Trials 159

    Pointing Breed Hunt Tests 160

    Other Dog Sports 160

CHAPTER 15

Grooming 163

Coat Basics 163

Essential Grooming Tools 164

Bathing 166

Brushing 168

Cleaning Eyes and Ears 168

Trimming Nails 170

Brushing Your Dog's Teeth 171

CHAPTER 16

Basic Health Care 173

Visiting the Vet 173

Allergies 174

Fleas and Ticks 176

Internal Parasites 176

Vaccinations 178

Spaying and Neutering 179
Holistic Alternatives 180
Pet Insurance 182

CHAPTER 17

The Aging Vizsla **183**

Basics of Senior Dog Care 183
Veterinary Care for Senior Dogs 185
Nutritional Changes 185
Exercising the Senior Dog 187
Household Changes 188
Preparing to Say Goodbye 189
Quality of Life 190
Grief and Healing 191

CHAPTER 1
The History of the Vizsla

The Origins of the Vizsla

The Vizsla dog breed was originally developed by the nomadic Magyar people, who traveled from the Ural Mountains of Russia to the Carpathian Basin sometime in the late ninth century. When the Magyars made their trek to the region now known as Hungary, they brought their beloved dogs with them. Primitive stone carvings dating to about 1,000 years ago show the Magyar hunters with dogs similar in type to the Vizslas of today.

When the Magyars arrived in Hungary, they changed their nomadic ways and settled down into a life of agriculture. They raised cattle, pigs, and horses

Photo Courtesy of Lexi Ryan

*Photo Courtesy
of Rayel Sorenson*

for food and agricultural work but still relied on hunting to provide food for their families. To accomplish this, they developed dogs that could scent out gamebirds while falcons were trained to retrieve them.

The Magyars' new homeland was invaded by the Turks in 1526. During the 150 years of Turkic rule that followed, the Magyars' favorite hunting dogs were crossed with the yellow pointers brought to the region by the Turks. It was at that time that the breed was named Vizsla, as the name meant "seek" in Turkish and "point" in Hungarian.

After the Turkic rule of Hungary ended, the German Hapsburgs took over, and only those in the upper class were allowed to inherit land. Hunting became a more organized sport, and hunters from other countries brought their own hunting dogs with them. Those dogs were eventually crossed with the now yellow dogs of Hungary, further refining them into the ideal hunting breed for birds and small game.

Most Hungarian hunters chose to keep the Vizsla pure for many generations to preserve their ideal type, but others continued to outcross to foreign breeds such as Pointers and Setters. In 1882, Hungarian hunters realized that they had very few purebred Vizslas left. They sought to re-establish the breed by introducing the Schweizhund, which was a solid red-colored hound with a powerful scenting ability.

FUN FACT
Vizsla Club of America, Inc. (VCA)

Founded in the 1950s as the Magyar Vizsla Club, the Vizsla Club of America (VCA) is the breed's American Kennel Club (AKC) parent club. The VCA has published its newsletter since 1953 and is now made up of 35 regional Vizsla clubs across the country. For more information about membership and events hosted by the club, visit www.vcaweb.org.

World War I and the Hungarian Peace Treaty brought unrest to the region, but many Vizsla breeders were determined to keep their breed alive and intact. The Magyar Breeding Association was formed in 1920 to hold field trials and develop a written breed standard. By 1941, many wealthy landowners had fled Hungary due to the start of World War II. It's believed that there were over 5,000 Vizslas registered in Hungary prior to the war, but after the Soviet invasion, approximately 80% of the breed's population had been lost. Additionally, important documents such as registrations, photos, and pedigrees were destroyed during that time.

The Vizsla first arrived in America in the 1950s. A female Vizsla named Sari and her two puppies, Shasta and Tito, were sent to Frank Tallman of Kansas City by a friend stationed in Italy. Several months after their arrival, Tallman requested another Vizsla and was sent a dog named Rex Del Gelsomino.

By the following year, more interested men were arranging for the purchase and shipment of Vizslas from both Austria and Germany. Dr. Ivan Osborn was responsible for importing over 40 Vizslas and became one of the main contributors to the breed in the United States. One of his first imports was named Broc Olca, who was imported from Czechoslovakia. Many modern Vizslas are able to trace their pedigrees back to this dog.

In addition to the Vizslas being imported into the United States, Hungarian refugees were arriving in large numbers, many bringing their beloved Vizslas with them. By 1953, the Magyar Vizsla Club of America had been established. Dedicated breeders and breed enthusiasts worked together to register 500 three-generation pedigrees with the American Kennel Club by 1960. That same year, the AKC officially recognized the Vizsla, placing the breed into the Sporting Group. At the time of its acceptance, the national breed club dropped Magyar from its name, officially becoming the Vizsla Club of America. Today, the Vizsla Club of America works to promote and preserve the Hungarian treasure known as the Vizsla.

The Vizsla's Influence on Other Breeds

Though there are many European hunting breeds that have somewhat murky histories, it is well-known that the Vizsla helped to develop the Weimaraner, Wirehaired Vizsla, and the German Shorthaired Pointer.

The Weimaraner is a German hunting dog that is sometimes referred to as the "Gray Ghost" due to its unique coat color. Though they are significantly larger than the Vizsla, it's easy to see the similarities in build and breed type. The Weimaraner was originally developed in the 19th century in Weimar, Germany, by Grand Duke Karl August. The duke sought to create his own ideal hunting breed by combining Bloodhounds with a number of French and German breeds. One of the most influential breeds in this mix was the Vizsla, which helped the duke's new breed by adding stamina, scenting ability, and elegance.

Though the Wirehaired Vizsla is similar in appearance to today's Vizsla, it is a separate breed. Hungarian hunters wanted a dog with a sturdier frame and denser coat to hunt in the frigid winters of northern Hungary. To accomplish this goal, they crossed their beloved Vizslas with German Wirehaired Pointers. The result was a larger, sturdier Vizsla with a wiry coat and distinctive beard and eyebrows.

The German Shorthaired Pointer (GSP) is another breed heavily influenced by the Vizsla. This breed was developed in the 19th century by German bird hunters who wanted a breed with powerful scenting ability and versatility. It's likely that the GSP descended from the now-extinct German Bird Dog. However, it was crossed with several other breeds in an effort to refine the breed and increase its natural hunting instinct. As with the Weimaraner, it's not too difficult to see the similarities between the GSP and Vizsla in terms of build, breed type, and athleticism.

It's also important to note that there is much conjecture regarding these breeds' influence on the Vizsla. Though the Vizsla's ancestors were used in the development of other breeds, it's believed that those same dogs may have been used to help re-establish the Vizsla at the end of the 19th century. At that time, the Vizsla's numbers were dwindling toward extinction, and it was necessary to broaden the gene pool in order for the breed to survive. However, there are no written records of this project, so it's still unknown whether the Weimaraner, Wirehaired Vizsla, or German Shorthaired Pointer may have been used to revive the Vizsla breed.

The Modern Vizsla

Today, the Vizsla continues to be the versatile athlete that the Magyars envisioned. The modern Vizsla can be seen competing in a wide range of dog sports, including hunting tests, field trials, conformation, obedience, rally, and agility. Many Vizslas have also successfully participated in tracking, barn hunts, and lure coursing. In 2000, a Vizsla named Legacy's DeChartay became the first dog of any breed to earn five AKC championship titles in different disciplines. Chartay, owned by Jack Sharkey, earned championship titles in conformation, field trials, agility, obedience, and hunting tests. Additionally, Chartay earned a spot in the prestigious Vizsla Club of America Hall of Fame.

Photo Courtesy
of Katie Higgins

Photo Courtesy
of Steve and Joan Shambaugh

Outside of the world of dog sports and shows, Vizslas can be seen making visits to hospitals, nursing homes, and libraries working as therapy dogs. They've also been employed by the Transportation Security Administration (TSA) as bomb-sniffing dogs. In fact, Vizslas are considered one of the top three breeds for explosive detection. Vizslas were also among the search-and-rescue teams that worked at Ground Zero after 9/11.

The Vizsla continues to be one of the most talented and versatile dog breeds in the world. In fact, the Vizsla Club of America (VCA) sponsors a Versatility Certificate program to encourage Vizsla owners to participate in a variety of disciplines. The program rewards owners for competing with their dogs in field, obedience, and conformation. Once a Vizsla meets these requirements, it is awarded a Versatility Certificate to acknowledge the dog's hard work and training. This program also has the benefit of bringing together new owners and experienced Vizsla people to appreciate everything this incredible breed has to offer.

CHAPTER 2
The Vizsla

Physical Characteristics

The Vizsla is a medium-sized, smooth-coated hunting breed with a distinguished appearance. They are lightly built yet still robust and capable of power and endurance. Vizslas are true working dogs and as such, are never penalized in the show ring for sinewy muscular condition, honorable scars, or field conditioned coats. Male Vizslas stand 22 to 24 inches at the shoulder and weigh between 55 and 60 pounds. Female Vizslas are slightly smaller at 21 to 23 inches at the shoulder, weighing 44 to 55 pounds. The Vizsla's overall appearance is that of an athlete capable of hunting in the field, forest, and water.

Photo Courtesy
of Diana Szogi

According to the breed standard, the Vizsla's head is lean, muscular, and moderately wide between the ears. The muzzle should be equal in length and slightly shorter than the skull when viewed from the side. The muzzle is also square and deep, tapering gradually from the skull to the tip of the nose. The nose should be the same color as the dog's coat, and a black nose is penalized in the show ring. Some Vizslas may have freckles from age or sun exposure.

FUN FACT
Hungarian Origins

The modern-day Vizsla is descended from ancient Hungarian hunting dogs. An early ancestor of the Vizsla is depicted in stone etchings of a Magyar hunter with his falcon and dog. Magyar clans occupied the land that is now Hungary beginning in the late ninth century.

The Vizsla's ears are thin and silky with well-rounded ends. They are proportionally long, low set, and hang close to the dog's cheeks. The jaws are well developed, and the teeth meet in a scissor bite. The Vizsla's eyes are medium size, and their color should match the dog's coat.

The Vizsla's neck is strong, muscular, and moderately long, leading into moderately laid-back shoulders. The body is strong, well-proportioned, and square. Vizslas never appear long and low or tall and leggy. The Vizsla's topline slopes gently from the withers to the croup. The chest is moderately broad and deep enough to reach the elbows. The ribs are well-sprung, and the underline exhibits a slight tuck-up.

The Vizsla's tail is thicker at the root than at the end. Docked tails are preferred. The ideal length for the tail is about a third docked off, as the tail should reach the back of the stifle joint. The Vizsla's legs are well developed and straight when viewed from the front or from behind.

Vizslas have a short, smooth coat that is dense and close-lying. There is no woolly undercoat, nor should the coat be distinctly long. The color is always golden rust, though the shade may vary. Sometimes, Vizslas may have lighter shadings over the sides of the neck and shoulders in an almost saddle-like appearance. Pale yellow and dark mahogany are not acceptable breed colors. A small amount of white on the chest and toes is permitted. Excessive white is a disqualification, but if the white is obviously due to aging or scarring, a judge will not penalize the dog. The Vizsla is a self-colored dog, meaning the eyes, eyelids, lips, nose, nails, and foot pads are the same color as the coat.

Behavioral Characteristics

According to the AKC breed standard, the Vizsla is a lively, gentle-mannered dog. They are demonstrably affectionate with their loved ones. Though fearless and naturally protective, Vizslas should never be shy, timid, or nervous. They have a natural hunting instinct, which is typically expressed through pointing or chasing. Some Vizslas may have a high enough prey drive that they cannot be trusted around small animals such as cats or chickens. They are a high-energy breed that requires plenty of daily exercise. Without adequate physical and mental stimulation, Vizslas are prone to developing boredom-related bad habits.

Vizslas are intelligent and highly trainable dogs. Psychologist Stanley Coren performed an in-depth study on canine intelligence and ranked the Vizsla as the 25th most intelligent dog breed out of the 79 breeds that

Photo Courtesy of Ashley Tucker

participated. Coren's study ranked breeds according to their responses to obedience training. The dogs were judged on how quickly they understood new commands and how frequently they obeyed the first command once learned. In many other studies, the Vizsla has been consistently ranked above average in terms of intelligence and trainability. Their trainability is part of the reason that Vizslas excel in such a wide range of disciplines and activities.

Vizslas as Family Dogs

> **"**
>
> *Vizslas thrive in the hub of family activity, so an active person or family that wants an active, social, and intelligent dog to join in on their adventures is ideal.*
>
> CAROL B PHELPS
> *Szizlin Vizslas, Reg.*
> **"**

The Vizsla is a people-oriented breed that truly adores its owners. At home, Vizslas are affectionate and are often described as "Velcro dogs" due to their preference for being as close to their owners as possible. They are typically gentle and friendly. Most Vizslas will also happily welcome a stranger into their lives as it's yet another opportunity for them to receive affection; however, some dogs may be more protective and bark at a stranger until properly introduced. Vizslas can be high-energy dogs, so some training and socialization are necessary for them to interact with small children and fragile older people. Vizslas are not a breed that can be left alone in the backyard for hours at a time. They prefer to be near their humans and will whine, bark, or become destructive if they feel abandoned or isolated.

The ideal family for a Vizsla is one that is active enough to provide sufficient daily physical and mental stimulation. Without enough exercise, Vizslas are prone to developing destructive behaviors out of boredom. If you don't keep your Vizsla entertained, he'll seek his own form of entertainment. Vizslas love spending time with their families, so the more activities you can do with your dog, the happier he'll be. This breed particularly enjoys outdoor activities such as hiking, mountain biking, and swimming. No matter what type of adventures your family goes on, a Vizsla will happily accompany you.

*Photo Courtesy
of John Brown*

Vizslas as Sport and Performance Dogs

If you're looking for a biddable and athletic sport or performance dog, look no further than the Vizsla. This breed is known for being incredibly trainable with the strength and endurance to perform in a range of disciplines. The Vizsla is a versatile breed capable of excelling in hunting tests, field trials, agility, obedience, rally, lure coursing, flyball, and more. Additionally, Vizslas are a popular choice for people competing in canicross and bikejoring.

If you're looking for a hunting dog, the Vizsla is ideal. Most hunters agree that this breed's preferred hunting style is at a medium pace and range. However, different bloodlines are bred for different purposes. Some lines of Vizsla may prefer to run faster and further than those used by foot hunters. Vizslas excel in upland hunting, though they aren't ideal for frigid waters. Many trainers claim that Vizslas' sensitive nature makes them softer dogs in terms of demeanor than other breeds, such as the German Shorthaired Pointer. However, their intense desire to please means that they're willing to do what it takes to make you happy. Additionally, their boundless energy and drive to work mean that they're happy to spend the entire day in the field with their favorite person.

Vizslas and Prey Drive

The Vizsla has been bred for centuries to point and retrieve game for their owners. This has resulted in a breed with a fairly high prey drive. Of course, prey drive varies by individual dog. Dogs from field-bred lines will likely have a higher prey drive than those bred for companionship or the show ring. However, Vizslas differ from other high-drive breeds as they are not typically allowed to chase and kill their prey. Vizslas are bred to have a "soft mouth," which means they need to retrieve game without damaging it.

Proper training and socialization can help Vizslas to understand which animals are okay to pursue and which ones they need to leave alone. Many Vizslas can live comfortably in a home with cats or small pets, while others may not be able to be trusted near these types of animals. If a high prey drive is a concern, it's best to discuss the matter with your breeder to make sure that you get the right Vizsla for your lifestyle.

Photo Courtesy
of Katie Bricker

Is the Vizsla Right for You?

> "
>
> *Vizslas are WONDERFUL dogs for some people, but definitely not a good choice for many others. The Vizsla is a highly active, sensitive, smart, demanding, compassionate, and needy companion. We cannot express that enough. They do very well in an active, devoted, and kind family that is ready to have a best friend and hip attachment. Basically, it is more like adopting a child, not having a dog. They require both mental and physical stimulation. An ideal home for a Vizsla is a home that is willing to dedicate LOTS of time and love by going on long walks/runs, trail bike rides, hunting, agility, tracking, or other activities.*
>
> PETER & LINDSAY SUGDEN
> *Sunchaser Vizslas*
>
> "

Determining whether a Vizsla is the right dog for you and your lifestyle is a decision that only you can make. However, there are a few things to keep in mind when determining whether a Vizsla is an appropriate choice. Most importantly, Vizslas are high-energy dogs that require a lot of physical and mental stimulation each day. If you are unable or unwilling to set aside enough time each day to keep your dog exercised, a Vizsla may not be for you. As noted earlier, Vizslas can also have high prey drives, so if you live in a home with cats, poultry, or pocket pets, you may need to reconsider or at least decide how to keep your new dog safely away from your existing pets. It's also important to remember that Vizslas have short coats, so if you spend a lot of time outdoors in frigid temperatures, you might need to find a different breed. Most Vizslas are happy to wear a coat in the winter if it means they can still participate in daily activities, but it's still an important aspect of Vizsla ownership to consider.

If you are an active person that is looking for a dog to keep you company while you run, bike, hike, or swim each day, a Vizsla would be a great choice of companion. With proper training and conditioning, Vizslas are capable of keeping up with you for hours at a time. Remember, these dogs were bred to spend all day hunting in the field. Additionally, if you're a hunter looking for a sensitive and biddable bird dog or a dog sport competitor searching for your next performance dog, you should certainly consider a Vizsla.

CHAPTER 3
Finding Your Ideal Vizsla

Purchasing from a Breeder vs. Adopting from a Rescue

When deciding where to find your new Vizsla, it's important to consider what kind of dog you're looking for. If you can develop an image of your ideal dog, you'll be better prepared to begin your search. If you intend to show your Vizsla, hunt with him, or compete in certain dog sports, your best bet is to find a breeder that does these activities with their own dogs. A pedigree filled with dogs titled in the sports you want to do will give you a better chance of success than bringing home a random dog from the shelter. That's not to say that rescued dogs are incapable of performing in these disciplines, but the odds are not in your favor. If you're simply looking for an active companion for your family, you may not need to be as picky about your new Vizsla's pedigree.

Purchasing a Vizsla from a reputable breeder is a great way to ensure that you're bringing home a healthy dog. It's important to remember that breeders don't just have puppies available. Many breeders will have adult dogs available on occasion, whether they are retired show dogs or dogs from past litters that have been returned to the breeder. It's essential that you do plenty of research on breeders and do not purchase from the first one you find on the internet. Do not sign any agreements or contracts until you're certain that breeders are working to improve the Vizsla breed with every generation and not just breeding to pad their pockets. Reputable breeders are likely to ask you just as many questions as you ask them, and they will never pressure you into purchasing one of their puppies. However, if you're interested in purchasing a Vizsla from a breeder, it's important

Photo Courtesy
of Chrys Longley

to understand that you may be placed on a waitlist for some time. Many reputable breeders only have one or two litters per year, and they can have a lengthy waitlist, so it's best to begin your search early rather than when you're in a hurry to bring a dog home.

When buying a purebred Vizsla, it's crucial that you purchase your dog from a reputable breeder rather than a pet store, puppy selling website, or backyard breeder. Dogs purchased from these sources typically come from puppy mills, which are commercial breeding operations that usually keep their dogs in horrific conditions. Although some facilities may claim that they are USDA licensed or professional breeders, their dogs are not treated humanely. It is entirely legal to keep a dog in a small wire cage for its entire life, so these facilities are operating within the confines of the law.

Additionally, puppy mills do not health test their dogs prior to breeding, so the dogs they produce are not bred to standard and can potentially have a myriad of genetic health problems. The puppies may have little to no vaccine history, and respiratory disorders, vision problems, and parasites are also common. What money you may save by buying a puppy from a puppy mill, you'll end up spending on veterinary care. It's also possible that puppies produced by commercial facilities are not purebred, though they may have papers anyway. This risk is especially high when breeders produce puppies with off-standard coat colors. Puppy mills also do not care about the temperaments of the dogs they produce, so puppies bought from mills frequently have behavioral issues such as aggression or fearfulness. While it may be cheaper, faster, or more convenient to buy a puppy from a pet store or a website such as Puppy Find or Craigslist, you will not end up with a healthy, high-quality Vizsla.

If you do not need a Vizsla for a specific purpose or are willing to take your chances on a dog with a potentially unknown past, you might consider purchasing your new Vizsla from a rescue organization or shelter. Getting a dog from a shelter does not mean you don't need to do your research, however, as there are plenty of shady rescue groups that don't always have the animals' best interest in mind. It's not common to find purebreds like Vizslas in most local shelters, but you might consider beginning your search with breed rescues. The Vizsla Club of America (VCA), for instance, has several rescue resources listed on its website. Breed-specific rescues are often a great place to begin your search as they have a better understanding of the unique needs and traits of Vizslas than your average local animal shelter.

THE BREEDER/OWNER RELATIONSHIP

By: Linda Maus – MausHaus Vizslas

I strongly suggest that every new Vizsla owner should select a breeder with whom you can develop a trusting and honest relationship with from the very start. Be forthcoming about the time you have for exercise and training and what your future intentions are.

Trust your breeder to select the best-suited puppy for your needs. As a breeder, I am with my puppies 24/7 and conduct temperament, conformation, and hunting evaluations. I do my best to match each puppy with its forever home based on puppy strengths and a new owner's requested traits.

 You meet the breeder and dam in person. Listen to how the breeder explains raising and training the puppies/dogs. You are getting years of expert advice from someone who cares deeply about the welfare of dogs.

 Inspect the housing location for cleanliness. It is imperative to have a clean and safe environment for whelping and raising puppies.

 Review the pedigrees and health testing of both dam and sire.

 Visit more than once so you get a feel for the temperament.

 Feel free to ask questions. Part of the responsibility of being a breeder is to educate and inform, especially new puppy owners. We are a resource available to you for the life of your dog.

Choosing a Reputable Breeder

If you've decided to purchase your Vizsla from a reputable breeder, it's essential that you don't buy a puppy from the first breeder you find. Even if there are breeders located in your town or county, it's important to expand your search to find the right breeder. The internet can be a great resource in aiding your search, but you'll need to do your research to distinguish the reputable breeders from the backyard breeders. Most reputable breeders will list their dogs' accomplishments on their websites or litter listings. This will include any titles earned in conformation or other dog sports. While an untitled dog is not necessarily a sign of a disreputable breeder, titled dogs prove that a breeder is producing quality puppies that are capable of performing in a variety of disciplines.

Most breeders are also more than happy to share their Vizslas' health test results. In most cases, these results are published on the Orthopedic Foundation for Animals' (OFA) website and can be located by searching the dog's registered name or OFA number. Any breeder that is unwilling to provide you with this information, or those that simply assure you that their dogs are healthy, are unlikely to be reputable breeders. The OFA recommends certain tests for each breed, so it's crucial that you make sure the breeder has tested for Vizsla-specific disorders. These tests will be discussed in-depth later in the chapter.

A great place to begin your search for a reputable breeder is the Vizsla Club of America's website. The VCA publishes a list of club contacts for each state or region of the country. By contacting the people on this list, you'll be able to get in touch with breeders recommended by the national and

Photo Courtesy of Linda Maus MausHaus Vizslas

Photo Courtesy
of Rayel Sorenson

regional breed clubs. One of the best ways to find a reputable breeder is to attend a local dog show or competition. This is especially true if you intend to compete with your new dog. At the competitions, you'll be able to speak to competitors who will not only be able to tell you more about the breed, but they'll also be able to recommend breeders. Furthermore, you'll be able to see the quality of dogs being produced by those breeders. Just remember that competitors are there to compete, so be sure to ask if they have time to speak to you before you begin asking questions. Most people are happy to discuss their dogs during their downtime between classes but may be in a rush if they're scheduled to go in the ring shortly.

RESCUE VIZSLAS

By: Linda Maus – MausHaus Vizslas

A rescue dog could have been surrendered for a multitude of reasons. Sometimes owners' lifestyles can change drastically (divorce, declining health, or even death) and they are unable to properly care for a dog anymore. The best thing owners can do for their beloved pets is to surrender them in hopes of finding a better placement. The breed rescue coordinator will know the particulars of why a dog was surrendered and should share information with you.

Things to consider when looking at a rescue dog:

 Health condition and vaccine history

 What was the dog's previous placement like? (with a family of children or a single adult owner)

 Does he/she get along with other pets?

 What level of training does he/she have?

Having this information will allow you to make an informed decision whether or not you wish to continue raising this dog.

Most importantly, spend some time with this dog before you make a final decision. Go for a walk together. Play fetch. Having the dog show his/her personality may just be what it takes to find your new best friend.

Remember, a reputable breeder always prioritizes the health and well-being of their dogs, as well as the breed as a whole. They breed to improve the Vizsla with every generation, while adhering to the breed standard. Reputable breeders do not breed for off-standard characteristics such as incorrect colors, sizes, or markings. Puppies with disqualifications may be produced on occasion, as is the nature of genetics, but good breeders do not knowingly breed dogs with health problems or off-standard features.

HELPFUL TIP
Keep Them Moving

Vizslas are incredibly high-energy dogs who love to stay active. Their high energy level makes Vizslas great companions for hiking, running, and possibly even biking. In addition, some Vizsla owners turn to dog sports to help their dogs expend their excess energy. So, if you're looking to bring a Vizsla into your home, plan to exercise your dog for about 60 minutes each day.

Reputable breeders also do not allow puppies to go to their new homes before the age of eight to twelve weeks. Additionally, reputable breeders are always interested in matching the right dog to the right person. They don't generally let buyers pick puppies based on appearance and instead will help buyers choose the right dog based on temperament and potential. If breeders do not ask you questions about your lifestyle and your goals for the dog, or they encourage you to pick a dog based solely on appearance, they are not reputable breeders.

Questions to Ask a Breeder Before Bringing a Vizsla Home

When interviewing breeders about their Vizslas, you'll likely be asked many questions about your lifestyle and what you want to do with your new dog. Breeders will want to not only make sure that the Vizsla is the right breed for you, but they'll want to make sure they can match you with the right dog. However, it's equally important for you to ask the breeder questions. Many buyers continue to have a close relationship with their dog's breeder, so it's important that you get to know them and make sure they're someone you can turn to if you ever experience any problems with your Vizsla in the future. Some of the questions you should ask include:

- How long have you been breeding, and what experience do you have with Vizslas?

- Are the dog's parents titled in any sports?
- Have any puppies from past litters gone on to earn titles or compete successfully?
- Will the dog you've matched me to have the right conformation and temperament for my goals?
- What health tests have been performed on the parents, and where can I see the results?
- How do you socialize your puppies?
- What vaccinations will the puppies have when they are ready to go to their new homes?
- Do you provide a health guarantee?
- Can I contact you about my puppy after I've taken him home?
- Do you require your buyers to sign a contract?

Remember, choosing the right breeder is an important part of ensuring that you get the right dog for your lifestyle. It's crucial to make sure you're getting your Vizsla from someone who cares for their dogs and will be a valuable resource for you to consult throughout your new dog's life.

Choosing a Reputable Rescue

> *When adopting from a rescue, you will want to find out as much as you can about the dog's history. There's usually a reason the dog has been rescued; most often the previous owners did not care, train, or provide for the needs of the dog. This will have a lasting effect on the dog's future behavior, which you will need to be prepared for.*
>
> **KATIE ALEXANDER**
> *Minnie Ridge Vizslas*

If you've decided to get your new Vizsla from a reputable rescue organization rather than a breeder, you'll still need to make sure you're working with the right people who will help you find the right dog. It's also important to understand that you'll still need to undergo a bit of scrutiny before being allowed to take your Vizsla home for the first time.

During the application process, it's crucial for you to be as honest as possible about your home and family. Most application forms will ask you about your house, yard, job, lifestyle, and finances. Some may even ask to view your home prior to approval. Remember, rescue staff or volunteers are not going to judge you; they are only interested in making sure the dogs go to their forever homes. It can be incredibly stressful and emotionally damaging for dogs to be taken to a new home only to be returned a few days, weeks, or even months later. To ensure that the dogs are not passed from home to home, most rescues just want to make sure you're the right fit.

It's also important to realize that it can take several days or even weeks before being approved for adoption. Many rescue organizations are run by volunteers and do not have the resources for quick approvals. This may mean that the dog you had your eye on may be adopted before you get approved. For this reason, it's generally recommended to fill out an application ahead of time and begin discussing your ideal Vizsla so that when a dog that fits that description comes into the rescue's care, you're already pre-approved for adoption.

Questions to Ask a Rescue Before Bringing a Vizsla Home

> When choosing a Vizsla, you are first choosing a breeder for the person's knowledge and continued support. Then you need to look at the bloodline for hunting, health, temperament, and conformation qualities. If you do that part correctly, then the breeder will guide you to the puppy that best fits your desires and home.
>
> **MARK AND PAM SPURGEON**
> *Crimson Sky Vizslas*

As with purchasing a Vizsla from a breeder, asking questions is an equally important aspect of purchasing a dog from a shelter or rescue organization. When you first apply for adoption or go to meet the dog, it can be overwhelmingly exciting, and it's easy to forget important questions in the moment. It can be helpful for many people to come up with a list of questions beforehand so that they don't forget everything the first time they see their new Vizsla's face. Examples of questions to ask rescue staff or volunteers include:

Photo Courtesy of Diana Szogi

- What is the dog's personality like?
- Has the dog been spayed or neutered?
- Is the dog up to date on vaccinations?
- Has the dog been dewormed since it arrived at the shelter or foster home?
- Does the dog have a history of any health problems?
- Does the dog get along with other dogs/cats/children?
- Has the dog ever displayed any aggressive behavior?
- How does the dog respond to new people/places/situations?
- Is the dog housetrained?
- Does the dog know any commands? If so, which ones?
- Does the dog have any known behavioral problems or bad habits?
- Does the dog have any dietary restrictions or specific food preferences?

It can also be helpful to ask questions about the dog's history and how it ended up at the rescue. Though many dogs end up in rescue through no fault of their own, it's worth asking about. Some Vizslas are adopted and then given up because of breed-specific traits such as high energy or prey drive, but others may be given up for more challenging issues such as fearfulness or aggression. Regardless of the reason, you'll want to know about any problems prior to bringing your new Vizsla home.

Contracts and Guarantees

If you plan on acquiring your new Vizsla from a reputable breeder, it's likely that you will be required to sign a contract prior to bringing the dog home for the first time. The contract is typically designed to prioritize the dog's well-being while also protecting both you and the breeder. It will specify which dog you're taking home, how much you're paying, as well as any stipulations made by the breeder.

As the buyer, signing the contract implies that you agree to accept the responsibility of caring for the Vizsla in question for the duration of its life. Some breeders may include clauses in their contracts regarding routine veterinary care, vaccinations, and spaying or neutering at an appropriate age. Many breeders require that Vizslas going to a pet home, rather than a show or performance home, be altered. Some breeders may also return a portion of the dog's purchase price upon proof of spaying or neutering. Since dogs are required to be intact to compete in conformation shows, if you're buying a show prospect, your contract may reflect that.

Depending on the breeder's dietary preferences, there may also be clauses regarding the quality of food you're required to feed. Most breeders have been caring for dogs long enough to know what works for their breed and their specific dogs, so they may require or simply suggest a certain type of diet. This is especially true for breeders that feed their dogs a raw diet. Breeders who raise puppies on a biologically appropriate diet often ask that buyers continue feeding such a diet once they bring their new Vizslas home.

Photo Courtesy
of Dawn Duckett

It's also common for the contract to state the breeder's obligations to the buyer. For instance, many breeders will guarantee that the puppy is free from disease and certain genetic conditions. This guarantee may cover the first year of the dog's life or its entire lifetime, but the duration will be listed in the contract. Since most reputable breeders test their dogs for common genetic issues prior to breeding, the risk of puppies developing these problems is typically quite low. However, it's still important to cover this topic in the contract, as well as what actions should be taken should the puppy test positive within the guarantee's period of coverage.

Reputable breeders are almost always willing to take a dog back no matter what happens, but some breeders may also offer buyers a refund or a replacement puppy if requested. This generally also applies to any other problem that may force the buyer to give up ownership. Whether buyers are moving across the country and cannot take the dog with them or simply can no longer care for it, the breeder will typically state whether they should be contacted first. Most breeders do this to prevent the dog from ending up in a shelter or in an inappropriate home.

Prior to signing the contract, it's crucial that you read each line and discuss any questions you may have with the breeder. Remember, the contract is a legally binding document, so you need to make sure that it reflects your best interests as well as those of the dog. Most reputable breeders are happy to explain their contracts to ensure that you understand what's expected of you and what you can expect from the breeder regarding your new Vizsla.

Health Testing and Certifications

> Look at breeders who are proud of their pedigree and know at least the first three generations and their accomplishments. Also make sure the dogs are health tested with a minimum of hips and elbows, and it's even better if they have a CHIC (Canine Health Information Center) number. Make sure the puppies are raised in an environment where they are exposed to the sights, sounds, and smells of a regular household. Socialization from birth and beyond is a key to success.
>
> JANET LAMAN
> *Valhalla Vizslas*

Photo Courtesy of Morgan Murphy

Reputable breeders will always test their Vizslas for common genetic conditions prior to breeding them. Health testing can be expensive, but they do so to better the breed and work toward eliminating certain conditions from the gene pool. Rather than breeding dogs that could potentially pass painful or even deadly diseases onto the next generation, reputable breeders will generally opt to spay or neuter any dog that tests positive for common genetic disorders.

Breeders typically submit their results for evaluation to the Orthopedic Foundation for Animals (OFA), which is one of the leading organizations in canine genetic research. The OFA runs a database with health test results from every recognized breed. Test results are generally submitted by owners, breeders, or their veterinarians and are evaluated for a nominal fee. The OFA's website lists recommended tests for each breed, as well as the recommended age for testing. For many tests, dogs must be over two years of age to have the results recorded. When all required and any optional tests are submitted for an individual dog, the results are kept in the OFA's Canine Health Information Center (CHIC), and the dog is assigned a CHIC number. Those results are publicly available and can be located by searching the dog's registered name or CHIC number.

For Vizslas, the tests required by the OFA include:

- X-rays for hip dysplasia

- Eye examination performed by a boarded ACVO veterinary ophthalmologist
- Autoimmune thyroiditis test – repeated annually up to 8 years of age

As previously stated, some tests are not required for a dog to receive a CHIC number, but they are recommended by the OFA. The optional tests recommended for Vizslas are

- Congenital cardiac evaluation performed by a board-certified veterinary cardiologist
- X-rays for elbow dysplasia
- Sebaceous adenitis testing performed by an approved dermatopathologist

Remember, reputable breeders are always willing to spend the money to fully health test their dogs prior to breeding to ensure that they are producing the healthiest Vizslas possible. They will never be shy about sharing those results with potential buyers, so if a breeder refuses to share that information, or you're unable to find the results in the CHIC database, it's recommended that you reconsider purchasing a dog from that breeder and continue searching for someone who is more upfront about the quality of their dogs.

For starters, the breeder must have done health testing on the bitch and have bred to a dog that has also had the health testing (hips, elbows, thyroid, cardiac, eyes). The reputable breeder proves his/her dog for structure, type, and temperament by showing. Ideally, the breeder also proves that the puppy parents know their job (hunting). The breeder should be involved with a breed club locally and or nationally. These are the clubs that protect the breed and support research.

JUDY HETKOWSKI
Boulder Vizslas

How to Choose Your Ideal Dog

Choosing your perfect Vizsla can seem like a daunting task, but it's important to seek the advice of people who know their dogs best. Breeders and rescue staff or volunteers know the dogs in their care better than anyone, which is why it's so important to discuss your ideal dog and your goals for that dog. Be sure to also discuss any potential dealbreakers to help the person match you to your ideal Vizsla.

It can be easy to get hung up on a dog's appearance. Vizslas are known for their charming, expressive faces, and it can be so easy to fall in love with a dog the first time you see it, especially as a puppy. However, just because you like a dog's appearance doesn't mean that it is the right dog for you. Even if you prefer a certain size, build, or shade of golden rust, it's crucial to keep an open mind. Temperament should always be your priority, though you may need more focus on appearance if you plan on showing your Vizsla in conformation. If that's the case, you'll also need to be on the lookout for any disqualifying or faulted markings or characteristics.

However, if you're looking for something as specific as a show or performance prospect, the breeder will be your best resource in matching you with the right Vizsla. In fact, many reputable breeders will not allow buyers to choose the puppy themselves, but rather they will match you to the ideal puppy once the dogs are old enough to begin showing personality and athletic capabilities. It's possible that the Vizsla you initially had your heart set on is not the right one for your lifestyle, so it's important not to get to attached to a dog until you're certain that it's the right one.

> *Let your breeder assist in selecting your dog. Be open to either sex unless there is a special reason for one over the other. Newbies should be open to either male or female. Over the years, you might enjoy adding the other sex. Vizslas are different—males and females. Experiencing both provides a lot of enjoyment and enhances your knowledge of the breed. Attempt to visit the litter often in the first two months. Your breeder spends every day with the litter, and you are able to view the early growth visit after visit. Some Vizslas are more active, curious, this one more reserved than that one, this one more focused on hunting, more appropriate for showing or other activities.*
>
> **STEPHEN J SHLYEN**
> *Rheingold Vizslas*

CHAPTER 4
Preparing Your Family for a Vizsla

> *Vizslas attach to all family members, unlike some other breeds who may pick one person in the family and perhaps not ignore but simply acknowledge all others. And if a member or two do fail to interact, the Vizsla may feel the stress. Be prepared for all members to want to establish a relationship—adults, children, and other animals. Observe a Vizsla going from person to person, learning communications from each. Welcome this special experience with your dog. There is an old Hungarian saying that goes like this: If you own a Vizsla, it lives on top of your head. Be prepared for this and enjoy the experience.*
>
> **STEPHEN J SHLYEN**
> *Rheingold Vizslas*

Yearly Costs of Owning a Vizsla

Regardless of your financial situation, it's crucial to understand the potential burden that Vizsla ownership can place on your finances. The yearly cost of owning a dog the size of a Vizsla is frequently much more than many people might expect. If you are already living on a tight budget, you may need to reconsider Vizsla ownership until you're financially in a more stable place. It can be easy to become enamored with the idea of bringing a dog into your home, but adopting a dog without the means to pay for its care is irresponsible. This section is not meant to imply that only wealthy people should own dogs; it's simply meant to prepare you for the possible costs you may face as a Vizsla owner. Dog ownership is entirely possible for most families with the right preparation and budget management.

Whether you choose to buy your Vizsla from a breeder or a rescue organization, you'll need to prepare for the up-front cost of the purchase price or adoption fee. Acquiring a dog from a shelter or rescue organization is typically less costly than getting a dog from a breeder, but you'll need to prepare for a fee of anywhere between $50 to $600 or more. The exact cost will depend on where you live and where the dog is coming from. Municipal shelters

Photo Courtesy of Tracy Mucci

HELPFUL TIP
Adopting an Older Vizsla

The Vizsla Club of America (VCA) recommends adopting an older Vizsla rather than a puppy for busy working couples or families with young kids. Vizslas are high-energy dogs that often act like puppies until they're around three years old. Housebroken older dogs may be easier to integrate into a family than a puppy. Older Vizslas can be found through rescues across the country. For a list of Vizsla rescues across the country, sorted by region, visit the VCA's website at www.vcaweb.org/resecue/contacts.shtml.

generally charge less for dogs than breed-specific organizations, but this is not always the case. Rescue dogs typically are not released to their new homes until they have been spayed or neutered and have all vaccines updated, so these services are generally included in the cost of adoption.

The price you pay for a Vizsla from a breeder will depend on the breeder as well as the specific dog's pedigree. Some breeders will charge less for pet quality dogs than they would for show or performance quality, but others may charge the same price regardless. You can typically expect to pay between about $1500 and $3000. If you're buying a finished hunting dog, you may expect to pay upwards of $8,500.

The price you pay to a breeder typically includes at least one round of vaccines and deworming, as well as tail docking. If you're purchasing an adult dog, he may already be up to date on vaccines or spayed or neutered, but it is possible that you may need to cover the costs associated with your new dog's initial vet visits. This price may seem like a lot, but it's important to understand that despite their prices, most reputable breeders make little profit from their litters. The income earned from a litter always goes toward health testing and titling dogs to ensure that they continue to produce high-quality Vizslas.

The initial purchase price of your Vizsla is likely to be the highest cost you face during the first few months of ownership, but you'll still need to budget for routine veterinary care and any supplies you may need. If you already have other dogs, your supply costs may be low as you likely already have most of what you need for your new dog. However, you'll still need to calculate the cost of feeding an additional dog as well as basics such as a new collar, leash, and identification tag. The cost of your first year of Vizsla ownership will vary according to your location as well as the quality of supplies you purchase, but you can generally expect to pay between $1065 and $3800.

Here is an approximate idea of the costs associated with your first year of Vizsla ownership:

Mandatory Expenses	Cost Estimate
Food	$300 - $900
Food and Water Dishes	$10 - $50
Treats	$50 - $150
Toys	$20 - $100
Collars and Leashes	$10 - $100
Crate	$50 - $200
Dog Beds	$50 - $350
Vaccines and Routine Veterinary Care	$150 - $500
Heartworm Testing	$10 - $35
Heartworm Prevention	$25 - $125
Flea and Tick Prevention	$40 - $200
Spaying and Neutering	$150 - $600
Puppy Classes	$200 - $500
Total	**$1065 - $3810**

Unfortunately, these are not the only potential costs you may face. Vizslas have relatively low- maintenance coats and require minimal grooming. However, many owners prefer having a professional take care of their dog's basic grooming needs, such as the occasional bath and nail trim. If you are unable or unwilling to groom your Vizsla at home, you'll need to include grooming costs in your budget. The price you pay will depend on the area you live in, but you can expect to pay a professional groomer anywhere between $30 and $80 for a full-service groom. It's worth noting that mobile groomers that come to your location typically cost more than groomers working out of a stationary salon.

Routine veterinary care is not the only medical cost that you may face in your first year of Vizsla ownership. Although most pet owners do everything they can to keep their dogs healthy and injury-free, accidents can and will happen, and you'll need to be prepared for the cost of emergency veterinary care. This can be a difficult cost to budget for, as the cost will depend on your dog's needs. An after-hours vet visit for something minor can run as little as a few hundred dollars, while a major emergency surgery can cost several thousand dollars. Pet insurance can help mitigate these costs, but it's not right for everyone. Insurance will be discussed in detail in Chapter 16.

Photo Courtesy of Emma Berry

Finally, if you frequently travel for work or pleasure, you'll need to make arrangements for your Vizsla's care while you're gone. Having friends or family care for your dog while you're away will be the least expensive option, but not everyone has this luxury. Boarding facilities will vary in cost according to the level of care they offer. For instance, a facility that offers a simple kennel with a few bathroom breaks per day will be less expensive than a facility that offers cage-free boarding, luxury kennels, or play groups.

Prices will also vary according to the area in which you live, but you can expect to pay between $30 and $100 per day. Many facilities also offer extra services such as grooming, training, or extra exercise or play time, so you'll need to include that in your budget if your dog requires extra care.

Possible Expenses	Cost Estimate
Professional Grooming	$100 - $500+
Emergency Veterinary Services	$200 - $2000+
Pet Sitting or Boarding	$15 - $80+ per day

As previously stated, this section is not meant to discourage you from Vizsla ownership; it's simply meant to prepare you for the possible costs associated with owning a dog. Bringing an animal into your home is a responsibility that should not be taken lightly. Remember, your Vizsla depends on you for everything from food and shelter to medical care and entertainment, so you need to make sure that you're able to provide your dog with the best care that you are able to afford. This may mean cutting back on other areas of your life or setting aside a small amount of money each month for emergencies. If you are truly committed to bringing a Vizsla into your home, this section will help you to prepare yourself financially for that commitment.

Preparing Children

Once you decide that you're ready to welcome a Vizsla into your home, you need to have a serious discussion with your children about their new family member. It can be tempting to surprise your kids with an adorable Vizsla puppy, but the surprise can be stressful and overwhelming for both the children and the puppy. By preparing your kids in advance, you can help them understand how their behavior will affect the new dog. Remember, frightened dogs may feel the need to lash out to protect themselves, so for the safety of everyone involved, it's best to prepare before you bring your Vizsla home for the first time.

Whether you're bringing home an adult Vizsla or a puppy, it's crucial to explain the need to be calm around the new addition. Depending on the age and size of the new dog, you may want your kids to sit or stand quietly and allow the dog to approach the kids rather than the other way around. By letting the dog sniff them before reaching out or approaching it, the dog is in control of its own space and will be less likely to react out of fear. If you're bringing home a puppy, it's generally recommended to have kids sit down for the initial introduction. This way, they won't tower over the puppy and frighten it or pick the puppy up, potentially putting the dog at risk of being dropped. Even a short fall from a child's arms can be enough to cause serious injuries to a puppy, especially to the head and neck, so it's safest for kids to interact with the puppy on the floor.

Depending on the age of your children, you may want to enlist them in the new dog's care. If your children are ready to handle tasks such as feeding or cleaning up after the dog, feel free to allow them to help. Caring for an animal can be empowering for kids and can teach them the importance of being responsible. However, don't forget to supervise when necessary.

You may also want to establish household rules for your new Vizsla prior to bringing him home for the first time. Discuss the rules with your children to ensure that they understand what is expected of them and the new dog when it arrives. If you don't want the dog on the furniture or you would prefer to keep him out of specific areas of the house, now is the ideal time to talk about it. This way, your entire family will be ready to enforce the rules consistently rather than trying to figure it all out with a rambunctious puppy underfoot.

Photo Courtesy
of The Neesen Family

Mutual Respect

While preparing for your Vizsla's first day in his new home, you need to consider how this decision will impact all members of your family, both human and animal. It's essential that everyone maintains a certain level of mutual respect, even when things are stressful. It can be hard work to ensure that each member of the family is as comfortable as possible, but it's crucial that everyone feels respected. If you have children or other pets, it's especially important to monitor all interactions with the new dog. Overstimulation is common with kids and pets, especially during the introductory period, and inappropriate play can happen quickly. Supervision is necessary to make sure that these instances do not escalate into an unpleasant or dangerous situation.

While you should always make sure that your new Vizsla is comfortable in his new surroundings, it's equally important to respect the boundaries of your kids and pets. Some pets may feel uncertain about the presence of a new animal in their home. This can be especially true if the animal has been the only one in the home for a long period of time. They may be unwilling to share their space or favorite items with the new dog. Kids may not appreciate the puppy stealing or chewing their favorite toys or having accidents in their bedrooms. This can lead to conflict if you aren't careful, so it's crucial that you ensure that everyone has their own space they can retreat to if they feel overwhelmed. Ideally, you should keep your Vizsla in a playpen, specific room, or kennel if you are unable to supervise him. Though this is an exciting period in your family's life, it can also be stressful, so it's important to do what you can to ensure that everyone feels included and respected.

Preparing Your Other Pets

Unfortunately, you can't explain the new arrival to your current pets in the same way that you would with children. But you can prepare a plan for introducing them properly. Proper introductions are especially important if you're bringing home an adult Vizsla or have particularly opinionated or dominant animals at home already. You should consider doing all introductions on neutral territory, if possible, to prevent your current pets from feeling the need to defend their turf. You may be able to do so at the rescue organization's facility or at the breeder's home, but this is not always possible. If you need to introduce them at home, try to do so in an area where your current pets do not spend much time, such as the front yard.

Photo Courtesy of Kristen Terech

Remember, Vizslas are a hunting breed, and many dogs have a strong prey drive. This can be evident at a young age, so it's important to be cautious when introducing a Vizsla of any age to smaller pets such as cats or pocket pets. Many Vizslas require a little bit of instruction before they can be trusted with other pets, while others may never be able to safely interact with smaller animals. Many species of pets can be kept safely in the same household without ever interacting with the dog if that is the safest option.

You will also need to be prepared for your current pets to be unwelcoming to the new arrival. Many pets can be stubborn and refuse to accept change at first, but they will warm up over time. For older pets or those that have been an only pet for a long time, they may require slower introductions and more space in the beginning. To prevent accidents or injuries, it's recommended to keep the animals separated until you're certain that they're willing to get along. Chapter 11 will go into more detail on bringing your Vizsla into a multi-pet household.

Family Commitment

Remember, adopting a Vizsla is a huge commitment, so it's crucial that you make sure every member of your family is on the same page prior to bringing your new dog home for the first time. Make sure that everyone agrees to getting a new dog and that they agree on a Vizsla. When you're ready to begin your search, it can be helpful for each member of the family to list their ideal characteristics to present to the breeder or shelter staff or volunteers. Each family member may also have a preferred role in

Photo Courtesy of Sara Gonzales

the new dog's care. Be sure to ask everyone about any concerns they may have about bringing a Vizsla into the home so that you can address them before committing to a certain dog.

If any family member disagrees with any part of this decision, you may need to step back and determine how you can proceed. Take the time to discuss any potential concerns in depth. They may simply need reassurance that they won't be doing all the work, or they may just have unanswered questions about the Vizsla breed or dog ownership in general. If necessary, you can redirect their concerns to the breeder or shelter staff for answers. Regardless of the problem, it's crucial that every member of the family is in agreement before you bring a Vizsla home.

CHAPTER 5
Preparing Your Home for Your New Vizsla

Creating a Safe Area Indoors

> " *Having a Vizsla puppy is a lot like having a baby. You will need to 'puppy proof' your home. Vizslas are a curious lot; they have a strong determination to explore their surroundings, especially if left alone. I suggest putting up baby gates to isolate the puppy in one room so it is safe and doesn't get into trouble. Vizsla puppies are active chewers, especially during teething. Shoes are a particular Vizsla favorite as they are usually on the floor and accessible, smell like their owner, and are made of leather. This is the trifecta for the perfect Vizsla chew toy.*
>
> **LINDA MAUS**
> *MausHaus Vizslas* "

Before you bring your Vizsla home for the first time, you should prepare a safe and comfortable area for him. If you already share your home with other pets, your home has likely already been pet-proofed, but it's still important to dedicate some extra time to keeping your newest family member out of trouble. Remember, puppies are incredibly curious and can often find trouble where you might not expect, so it's important to go over the area thoroughly. The other important reason for setting up a confined area for your new Vizsla is because it's likely that he may become overwhelmed in the first few days or weeks in his new home, and the safe space will provide him with an area to retreat to and rest. Plus, you'll have somewhere safe to place the dog when you are unable to supervise him closely.

The best areas for a new puppy are those that can be cleaned easily. Laundry rooms, bathrooms, or even sections of a kitchen tend to work well. You don't need a large space, especially if your new Vizsla is not yet house-trained. Smaller quarters will generally discourage a dog from relieving himself indoors as most dogs choose not to go to the bathroom near their sleeping or eating areas. Regardless of the space you choose, it's almost guaranteed that your Vizsla will make at least a few messes, so avoid car-peted areas if possible. If carpet is your only option, consider setting down

Photo Courtesy
of Christina Hughes

a waterproof barrier beneath a playpen or crate. You should also choose an area where your new dog will be able to watch the daily activities of his new family without being in the way. Secluded areas should be avoided as they will only cause undue stress. Ideally, your Vizsla's space should allow him to feel like he's part of the action but without being underfoot.

Your biggest priority in setting up your Vizsla's area should be safety. You need to choose an area that can be secured well enough that the dog cannot escape. Remember, Vizslas are intelligent and agile dogs, and it may surprise you how creative they can be in escaping if they think they're missing out on any fun. This is especially true of adult dogs. Make sure any barriers you erect are solid and unable to be jumped or pushed over. Free-standing barriers and feeble baby gates are not recommended. Eventually, you'll be able to train your Vizsla to respect flimsy barriers, but before you reach that point, your barriers may take some abuse. Pressure-mounted baby gates, heavy-duty playpens, and crates are often great choices. Improperly installed or flimsy barriers can result in injury or damage to your home or belongings, so it's crucial that you make sure the area is secure before leaving your Vizsla unsupervised.

Photo Courtesy of Diana Szogi

Necessary Supplies

Prior to your new Vizsla's arrival, you should make a list of necessary supplies to ensure you have everything you need for your first few days or weeks together. If you already have a multi-pet household, you may not need much, but making a list can help you visualize what you may or may not need. This is especially important if your current pets do not share well with others. By preparing in advance, you'll also prevent the need for any late-night emergency trips to the pet store after you've picked up your new dog.

HELPFUL TIP
Orthopedic Dog Beds

Orthopedic dog beds have flooded the pet goods market, but are they worth the extra cost for your Vizsla? A good-quality memory foam dog bed can be particularly beneficial to older dogs who suffer from arthritis or joint pain. Some sources indicate that using a memory foam dog bed for younger dogs can promote joint health. Vizslas can be prone to hip and elbow dysplasia as they age, which might be a factor to consider when choosing a bed for your new dog.

Food – It's not uncommon for new dog owners to thoroughly prepare for a puppy's arrival only to find that they've forgotten to buy dog food. Although it's one of the most important supplies to have on hand, it's also one of the easiest to forget. It's always a good idea to ask the breeder or shelter staff or volunteers what type of food your new Vizsla is currently eating. You may choose to continue feeding the same food or switch to a different diet, but consider purchasing a small amount of the old food to help make the transition easier on your new dog's stomach. Don't forget to ask about any food sensitivities or allergies so you can also pick up appropriate treats to begin training.

Collar, leash, and identification tag – If you already have other dogs in your home, you may be able to borrow a collar and leash for your new Vizsla, but it's more likely that you'll want to get your new companion something special. Most types of collars are somewhat adjustable, so if you aren't sure what size to buy, you should be able to estimate and adjust accordingly. Your local pet store or favorite online retailer likely has a wide selection of collars to choose from. Whether you prefer nylon, leather, or biothane, you should be able to find a collar in your preferred color or pattern. You will also have several styles to choose from, including flat collars, martingales, and slip or limited-slip collars. Whichever style you choose, don't forget to pick up a leash to match. You should also purchase an identification tag for your new dog. Though he may already be microchipped, having a tag with your phone number or address will be helpful should your Vizsla manage to get away from you during his first few days in his new home.

Dog bed – Until you get to know your Vizsla better, it's generally recommended to purchase a relatively inexpensive bed. If he's still a puppy, it's likely that he will outgrow the bed or chew it up during teething. Some dogs also prefer certain styles of bed over another, so it would be a shame to buy your dog a style that he won't use. Older Vizslas may prefer thicker beds or those made from memory foam for better support. Once you know your Vizsla's preferences better and are more certain that he won't destroy a nice bed, you can invest in a higher-quality dog bed. No matter what bed you buy, choose one with a removable cover that can be washed separately. It's much easier to toss the cover in the wash than the entire bed.

Photo Courtesy
of Nancy Barrows

Bowls – If you don't already have dogs in your home, you will need to purchase food and water bowls for your Vizsla. Your favorite pet store or website likely has a wide range of choices, including stainless steel, ceramic, plastic, and even glass. Durable materials such as stainless steel will likely last longer than cheap plastic, but the choice is yours. If you travel frequently, you may also want to invest in bowls that are easy to transport.

Toys – Though toys are not a necessary item to have before you bring your Vizsla home, most owners choose to have at least one or two toys available to help welcome a new dog into their new home. The type of toy your Vizsla will prefer will depend on his own unique personality. Some Vizslas enjoy durable chew toys, while others prefer something soft and squeaky. It's always helpful to buy a few different kinds until you learn more about your dog and his preferred style of play.

Grooming supplies – If you plan on grooming your Vizsla at home rather than taking him to a groomer, you'll need to add a few supplies to your shopping list. Even if you would prefer to have a professional groom him, you may still want to have a few supplies on hand should he get into something smelly on your groomer's day off. Plus, the more handling you do at home, the better behaved he'll be for the professionals.

A soft-bristled brush or rubber curry brush will help remove dead hair and dirt while also providing your Vizsla with a nice massage. Shampoo or waterless shampoo spray will also be appreciated the next time your dog decides to splash through mud puddles. If you want to trim your Vizsla's nails at home, you'll need either a nail clipper or grinder. Of course, there are plenty of other tools you may choose to have in your grooming kit, but these are just the basics. If you have any doubts about what grooming supplies work best with Vizslas, ask your local groomer for advice. Vizsla grooming will be discussed more in-depth in Chapter 15.

Housetraining supplies – Whether you're bringing home a puppy or an adult Vizsla, it's likely that you'll be cleaning up at least a few messes, so it can be helpful to have the right supplies on hand when they happen. Even the most well-trained dog can have an accident when he is under the stress of moving into a new home. Disposable or reusable puppy pads are a must-have item, especially if your Vizsla has not yet been housetrained. Cleaning supplies, such as enzymatic floor cleaners, will also be helpful in ensuring your dog doesn't return to the same place to relieve himself time and again.

Some owners also choose to buy a bell or string of bells to place on or near the door. Vizslas can be easily trained to paw at or nudge the bells with their nose to indicate their need to go outside. One of the most important housetraining items to have ready for your new Vizsla is an appropriately sized crate. This will not only aid in housetraining but will help keep your Vizsla out of trouble when you're unable to supervise him.

Basic Shopping List for Your Vizsla

- Food
- Collar and leash
- Identification tag
- Crate
- Bedding
- Food and water bowls
- Treats
- Toys
- Combs or brushes
- Shampoo
- Nail trimmer
- Puppy pads
- Cleaning supplies

Remember, this is not an exhaustive list, but it is a good place to start. All of the items on this list are available at a wide range of price points, so choose your items according to your budget. Additionally, if you have other dogs at home already, you may be able to forgo many of the items on this list.

Crates and Crate Training

Whether you're bringing home an adult Vizsla or a puppy, crate training will be an essential part of your first few weeks together. Though it's possible that your Vizsla may have had some experience with crates in his previous home, it's more likely that you'll be introducing the concept for the first time. You may not be interested in crating your Vizsla once he's responsible enough to be trusted with unsupervised access to your home, but it's still a crucial part of his training as he will eventually need to rest quietly in a crate or cage at the groomer or vet.

Without proper crate training, a Vizsla is at risk of hurting himself or those around him. Without training, most dogs will need to be physically pushed into the crate, and they may panic once inside. Excessive barking, digging, and chewing at the crate bars are common signs of a lack of crate training. This can result in a dog with broken teeth or nails or even lacerations. It also makes it difficult for veterinary professionals or groomers to do their job if they must constantly supervise your dog to ensure he doesn't hurt himself. A panicked dog may lash out at those around him once he is let out of the crate. To prevent undue stress and injuries, it's crucial to teach your Vizsla that the crate is a safe place for relaxation.

Additionally, the crate gives your Vizsla a place to retreat to should he feel overwhelmed by the activity in his new home. Vizslas are sensitive dogs and can become overwhelmed during the hustle and bustle of everyday life if they're not used to it. With proper training, your Vizsla will learn that he can retreat to his crate any time he feels like it. This is especially useful if you travel frequently with your Vizsla as the crate will provide him with a home away from home no matter where you go.

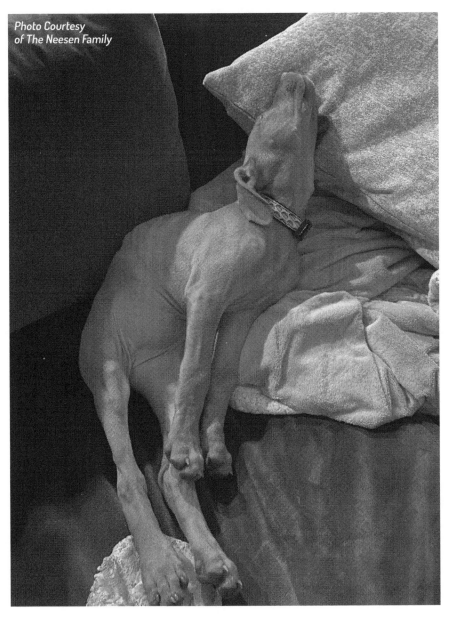

Photo Courtesy of The Neesen Family

Before you begin crate training, you'll need to decide what type of crate to use. Crates may be made of metal, wood, or plastic. Typically, wood crates are meant to be more decorative than functional and will not stand up to a destructive Vizsla puppy. Metal crates may be made of wire or metal panels. Wire crates tend to be quite inexpensive, but the ones made with metal panels will hold up best to destructive dogs. Plastic crates are also inexpensive, and many are approved for air travel. The type of crate you choose will depend on your individual dog, as well as your own preferences.

After deciding which type of crate you'd like, you'll need to choose the correct size. This can be difficult, particularly with a growing Vizsla puppy. A crate should be big enough to allow your Vizsla to stand up, turn around, and lie down comfortably. You don't want to choose a size that's too large either, especially if you're working on housetraining. A crate that's too large may encourage a dog to use part of the crate as a bathroom. For growing puppies, you may want to go with a wire crate with a divider that you can use to adjust the size of the crate as the dog grows. Otherwise, you may be buying a new crate each time your Vizsla outgrows the last.

To make the crate as appealing as possible, it's recommended to place your Vizsla's favorite bedding and toys inside. However, if your Vizsla is known for destroying things, you may need to have him stay in an empty crate. Otherwise, he could swallow a piece of toy or bedding and end up at the vet with an intestinal blockage.

You can begin crate training by tossing a few high-value treats into the crate. At first, your Vizsla may reach inside to quickly grab the treats before backing out. That behavior should be expected and not punished. Do not immediately lock your dog inside the crate, or he may panic. Instead, reward him for spending a few seconds longer inside the crate each time. As he becomes accustomed to the crate, you can shut the door briefly before opening it and rewarding him. However, do not reward your Vizsla for whining or barking while in the crate. If you let him out while he's having a tantrum, you're only rewarding him, and he'll be more likely to repeat this behavior in the future. Allow him to settle down before you open the crate door.

As he becomes more comfortable in the crate, you can introduce proper crate manners. Ask your Vizsla to wait a moment before releasing him. You can use a release word such as "okay" to let him know when he's allowed to leave. If your Vizsla attempts to leave the crate before you release him, simply place him back inside the crate and try again. Remember, positive reinforcement such as high-value treats and plenty of praise will help him to understand your expectations.

Dog-Proofing Your House

> *Their superior intelligence and ability to problem solve can make them incredibly easy to train and they become very fast learners, but left to their own devices, they rarely make good choices! That means you secure your trash cans, keep your counters clear of food, and check your fence! It's much easier to prevent naughty behaviors than it is to fix them, so you need to have puppies 100% in your line of sight until they begin making good choices!*
>
> **MICHEL BERNER**
> *Mira Vizslas*

After you've prepared an area in your home to keep your Vizsla safe and secure, you'll want to go through your home room by room to dog-proof it. If you already have other pets in your home, it's likely that you've already taken care of any significant dangers. However, your current pets may be used to the way things are and may overlook certain things that a curious new dog will not. This is especially true if you're bringing home a puppy. Puppies love getting into trouble and can often find it where you may least expect it. By going from room to room, down at the puppy's level, you'll be able to spot potential dangers that you may otherwise overlook. Though you won't be leaving your puppy unsupervised with access to your entire home, it's still best to make sure there are no serious dangers. Once you've properly dog-proofed your indoor space, you'll need to move outside to your yard or garden and repeat the process there.

Indoor Dangers

As you begin dog-proofing your home, perform this process one room at a time to ensure you don't miss anything. One of the best places to start is the kitchen, as it is often home to a wide range of potential dangers. The most dangerous item in your kitchen is probably your trash can. Trash cans contain any number of dangerous items, including broken glass or plastic, batteries, plastic wrappers or bags, and toxic food. Unfortunately, getting into the trash is a self-rewarding bad habit, so once a dog gets into it and finds a tasty treat, he's more likely to try again. Therefore, it's best to prevent your Vizsla from having that opportunity in the first place. If you cannot place your trash in a closet or cabinet, consider investing in a heavy dog-proof trash can. Many manufacturers make trash cans for this purpose, and some trash cans can even be locked for safety when you're not around to supervise.

Another potential danger in your kitchen is cleaning supplies. Though most people store their cleaning supplies in a closet or cabinet, some Vizslas are clever enough to figure out how to open doors to get into trouble, especially if they've been left unsupervised. To keep your new Vizsla out of trouble, consider placing your cleaning supplies on a high shelf where he cannot reach. You may also consider installing cabinet locks like those designed to keep children out.

The same caution should apply to the bathroom and any cleaning supplies you may have stored there. You should also be careful about any medication or beauty and hygiene supplies you may have in the bathroom. Vizslas are not large dogs, but many are tall enough to skim the edges of your countertops, so it's best to keep any dangerous items further back or stored up out of reach. If your bathroom has a small trash can, make sure that it's been safely stored away in a cabinet or placed on a countertop away from the dog.

In areas such as the living room or your home office, be sure that any electrical cables are stowed out of reach. Plastic zip ties are an easy and inexpensive way to keep cords from dangling and tempting a curious puppy. If you keep any valuable or sentimental furniture in these rooms, consider moving them somewhere safer or blocking off the room entirely until you're certain that your new Vizsla can be trusted not to chew or destroy. Window coverings such as curtains or blinds may also need to be altered to prevent your puppy from chewing and pulling them down.

Whether you're an avid indoor gardener with a plethora of houseplants or just have one or two for decoration, be very cautious about keeping plants where your Vizsla could come into contact with them. Both the ASPCA and AKC have lists on their websites of common houseplants that are toxic to dogs. Make sure that you remove any potentially toxic plants out of your Vizsla's reach. Even if your plants aren't toxic, you'll still want to make sure your puppy can't reach them. Otherwise, you'll find yourself cleaning up a mess of soil and chewed-up plant. Additionally, just because a plant isn't toxic doesn't mean it won't cause digestive upset.

As you move on to dog-proofing the bedrooms, make sure there isn't anything on the floor that can be chewed or swallowed by your new Vizsla.

*Photo Courtesy
of Haylene de Jager*

Clothing and shoes should be picked up and placed in closets or drawers. In your children's bedrooms, remove any toys from the floor and store them somewhere out of the puppy's reach. Remember, it takes only a moment for a dog to swallow a sock or small toy, but it could result in an expensive vet bill or tragedy if your dog chokes on the item or it causes an intestinal blockage. Again, you'll also want to make sure that any houseplants and electrical cords are moved away from the puppy's reach.

Another common indoor danger that could potentially cause your Vizsla harm is stairs. The risk of injury is even higher if you're welcoming a puppy or senior Vizsla into your home. Young and old dogs often don't have the strength to catch themselves should they lose their balance navigating the stairs. If you have more than a few steps in your home, consider investing in a baby gate or similar barrier. Baby gates can be permanently installed, or you can buy pressure-mounted gates that do not damage the surrounding walls. These types of barriers are typically easy for humans to open and close but cannot be opened by a dog when shut properly. However, if your Vizsla is a jumper, he may still be able to clear the barrier, so you'll need to spend some time training him to respect the barrier.

Outdoor Dangers

After you've finished dog-proofing your house, you'll need to move on to your outdoor space if you have one. Yards and gardens are also full of potential dangers, especially if you're bringing home a curious Vizsla puppy. The most important step in dog-proofing your yard is to walk along the fence line and make sure there are no holes or gaps, loose boards, rotted wood, or broken hardware. Puppies tend to accidentally find their way out of the yard, while adult dogs may actively search for a way out, so it's important that the yard is secure. You'll also need to make sure that the fence cannot be dug under or climbed or jumped over by your Vizsla. Remember, an escaped dog could easily be injured or killed by traffic or wild animals. Additionally, there's always the risk of your Vizsla running into humans with bad intentions.

Once you've examined your fence, move on to your plants. Just as you did indoors, you'll need to make sure that none of the plants present in your outdoor space are toxic to dogs. If they are, decide whether to remove them entirely or fence them off. If you have a vegetable or flower garden that you'd prefer to keep safe, you may also want to consider adding a temporary or permanent barrier. You can eventually train your Vizsla to stay out of certain areas, but it will be easier to erect a barrier until training is complete.

If you use chemical pesticides or fertilizers in your yard, make sure your Vizsla cannot ingest them. You may store such chemicals in an outdoor shed or garage, but you'll also need to make sure that those areas are closed off and cannot be accessed by your dog. Garages and sheds may also contain other hazardous chemicals such as antifreeze. Antifreeze poisoning is common with pets as it has a sweet taste. If ingested, antifreeze can cause kidney damage and death, so it's important to make sure you clean up any spills and store containers safely.

Finally, if your home has a pool, make sure that your Vizsla cannot access it without supervision. If it has a fence around it, make sure that your Vizsla cannot squeeze through. If the bars of your pool fence are too wide and your puppy can fit between them, consider installing a temporary barrier around the base. Chicken wire is an inexpensive choice that is easy to install. Once your Vizsla is large enough that he can no longer squeeze between the bars, you can always remove the chicken wire.

If your pool is not fenced, make sure that your Vizsla is never allowed outside without proper supervision. Even a well-trained adult dog may panic if he accidentally falls in and may be unable to find the way out. If you plan on swimming with your Vizsla in the pool, be sure to spend plenty of time teaching your dog where the stairs are and how to get out. However, no matter how well trained your Vizsla is, it's still best to supervise him during any pool time.

CHAPTER 6

Bringing Your New Vizsla Home

> ❝
>
> *I tell puppy buyers all the time that training a Vizsla is easy if you're smarter than a dog. If the dog happens to be smarter than you, then you'll be the one getting trained. Use simple one-word commands. Be consistent, be repetitive, and be kind. You'll be amazed at how quickly your Vizsla catches on.*
>
> **DENZIL RAY COOPER**
> *Cooper's Redneck Kennel*
>
> ❞

Planning Your Vizsla's Arrival

Welcoming a new dog into your home can be a stressful event, so it's important to plan your Vizsla's arrival in advance. Planning will help eliminate any last-minute panic when you realize that you've forgotten something important. It's impossible to completely eliminate the stress during the first few days with your Vizsla, but a thoroughly developed plan will set you up for success so that you can focus more on developing a relationship with your new companion.

As previously stated, you should already have the supplies you need at home before you pick your Vizsla up from the breeder or shelter. You should also have set up a secure space dedicated to your Vizsla and thoroughly dog-proofed your home. The next step in preparing for your new dog's arrival is to gather your family and decide what boundaries you want to set. Discuss topics such as whether you want the dog on the furniture, where he will sleep for the first few weeks, and who will provide what care.

Developing a Schedule

> *Have a structured schedule and routine. They love routine! Start teaching and learning immediately. New tricks, commands, experiences, and places! Do not let them manipulate you! Stick to your guns with crate training, meals, potty training, nail dremeling, and other routines.*
>
> CATHY GALLAGHER
> *Sienna Pointe Vizslas*

Before you bring your new Vizsla home from the shelter or breeder, it's recommended to develop a daily schedule or at least some idea of what your daily schedule will look like. This will help your new dog, as well as your family, adjust to a new way of life. Remember, if you're adopting a puppy or an untrained adult, you'll need to take the dog out every few hours for bathroom breaks. This may require some flexibility and coordination among your family members. It may be helpful to decide who will deliver the dog's daily meals and who will be responsible for bathroom breaks at various times during the day.

Many families find it helpful to write down their weekly schedule to better visualize what life with a new Vizsla will look like. Writing down your daily work schedules, appointments, and weekly obligations will help you to determine who will be available to care for the new dog when needed. You may also consider assigning each family member certain duties, though young children will need to be supervised if they are expected to contribute to your Vizsla's daily care.

By establishing a schedule beforehand and assigning roles to your family members, you'll hopefully be able to eliminate those frustrating moments that occur when the dog is given two dinners or a morning walk is forgotten. Most of the time, these occasions won't hurt your Vizsla, but it can be difficult to establish household rules without consistency.

Picking Your Vizsla Up from the Breeder

As long as you've done your homework and have thoroughly prepared your home for the arrival of your new Vizsla, picking up your new companion should be relatively uneventful. In the days leading up to your scheduled

Photo Courtesy of Krystal Hayes

pickup day, give your home a once-over to ensure that everything has been dog-proofed and you have everything you need for the first few days or weeks with your Vizsla.

If you haven't yet signed the breeder's contract, now is the time to go over the document one more time to make sure that all of the information is accurate and you understand everything you're agreeing to. You've likely already paid at least a deposit, so if you haven't yet paid the full purchase price, be sure to prepare cash or a check in the amount of your outstanding balance. This information is likely mentioned in the contract, so be sure that the stated amount is correct.

Finally, if you have any remaining questions for the breeder about your new dog, or the Vizsla breed in general, it's a good idea to write them down, send the breeder a quick email, or call them. If you make a mental note to ask later, you may forget once you have a charming red puppy in your arms. However, if you do forget to ask, don't panic. A reputable breeder will be happy to stay in touch after you've picked up your puppy and will gladly answer any questions you may have as they arise.

Bringing Your Vizsla Home from the Rescue

The process of picking up your new Vizsla from a rescue organization or foster home will be similar to picking him up from a breeder. Again, you should go through your home and make sure you're truly ready for the arrival of your new family member. Go over your shopping list and make sure you've got the basics. You can always run to the store later, but it's best not to stress out a new dog with a trip to the pet store immediately after being picked up from the shelter.

Additionally, the rescue organization you're working with will probably require you to sign a contract or adoption agreement, so you may want to go over it once more to ensure that you understand what is expected of you. If you are responsible for any veterinary care such as vaccines or spaying or neutering the dog, you'll need to know before you pick the dog up. Be sure to prepare cash or a check in advance to cover your new Vizsla's adoption fee. Finally, if you have any unanswered questions about your new Vizsla, be sure to write them down. Some rescues will stay in touch after adoption, but some may leave you more or less on your own after adoption, so it's best to ask now just in case.

The Ride Home

> 66
>
> *Remember, the pup has been with the mom, littermates, and breeder for its whole life and will likely be quite sad and lonely. We suggest getting a Snuggle Puppy–type stuffed animal with a heartbeat and heat pack. This is soothing and emulates being with the littermates. We also suggest that the new owners bring a blanket with them to rub on the mother, the breeders, the littermates, etc., when they pick up the pup. This helps the dog to adapt to its new environment with the familiar smells. The pups often will cry with the separation. The pup will need plenty of attention, love, and care.*
>
> **PETER & LINDSAY SUGDEN**
> *Sunchaser Vizslas*
>
> 99

As you prepare to bring your Vizsla home for the first time, it's important to understand that your new companion, regardless of age, may have little

FUN FACT
Born That Way

Vizslas are all born with blue eyes due to a lack of melanin in their bodies. The puppies usually open their eyes around two weeks of age, and their eyes start changing to amber around four weeks old. Adult Vizslas are universally a reddish-brown color with eyes to match. By the time you bring your puppy home at about eight weeks old, his eyes should be well on their way to their adult color, but each dog is different, and it could take up to 11 months for this change to occur.

to no experience riding in a car, so you need to be prepared for all possibilities. Your new dog will also be in the company of total strangers, away from his mother and littermates or foster home, so he'll likely be stressed already. In order to set your Vizsla up for a successful trip, it's important to remain as calm as possible during the ride home. Excitement could potentially escalate any fear he may experience, so you must lead by example.

Before you pick your Vizsla up, you'll need to decide on a safe method of restraint. An unrestrained dog in a car is a danger to himself and others, so it's important that you keep everyone safe. It's tempting to drive home with your new puppy in your lap, but this is not ideal. Even if your puppy doesn't panic, he could become car sick, which will be a hassle to clean up if you aren't prepared. The most common method of restraint during car travel is a kennel, but you may also use a seat belt or barrier. Kennels are popular because many dogs find them to be calming, as they provide an almost den-like space. If you're able to bring a small token from the dog's previous home, such as a blanket or toy, it may provide additional comfort. However, if you drive a particularly small vehicle, you may be more inclined to use a doggie seat belt and harness or a metal barrier. Whichever method you choose, be sure to prepare it ahead of time so that it's ready for your Vizsla's ride home.

Many dogs who aren't experienced with car travel can experience motion sickness, though some experienced travelers may also get sick on occasion. It can be stressful for everyone in the car to drive home after a dog has gotten sick, especially if it's a long drive. However, if you're prepared to clean up the mess, you can easily pull over and take care of the situation. Many owners choose to line their dog's kennel with disposable or reusable puppy pads or towels. Even small blankets will work well. If you're using a different method of restraint, consider buying a waterproof seat protector or cargo cover to help keep your car clean. Don't forget to bring a plastic bag or storage container to store soiled linens until you're able to wash

Photo Courtesy of Chrys Longley

them. If possible, ask the breeder or shelter volunteers not to feed your Vizsla just before your drive. That will help minimize the possibility of any motion sickness.

If the ride home will be your Vizsla's first time in a car, it's possible that he may react out of fear. Although most dogs react fearfully by shaking nervously, whining, or even barking, some may panic or attempt to escape the car. This is one of the many reasons to keep your Vizsla safely restrained in the car. A panicking, unrestrained dog in the car is a recipe for disaster. Whether your Vizsla rides calmly in the vehicle or reacts with extreme fear, it's crucial that you remain calm no matter what. If you get upset or try to coddle him, your Vizsla will believe that there is a reason to be afraid. You must show your new companion that there is nothing to be afraid of, so be the calm and confident leader that your Vizsla needs.

The First Night Home

It's generally not recommended to bring a new dog home the night before an important meeting or a busy day at work. Your first night with your Vizsla probably won't be very restful, so consider picking up your new companion on the weekend or before your day off. This is true for both puppies and adults, though puppies tend to have more sleepless nights than adults since this will be their first time away from their mother and siblings.

It's generally recommended to keep your Vizsla near you during the first few nights at home. Isolation may help you get a few more hours of sleep, but it can be stressful for a dog to be alone in a new house, especially if he's never been left alone before. If possible, set up a crate or playpen near your bed or at least in your bedroom. Even if you believe that your new Vizsla is fully housetrained, it's best to have him sleep in a small area at first to reduce the risk of him relieving himself indoors during the night.

Your first night at home with your Vizsla is your first opportunity to implement your new nightly routine, so make sure you take him outside to relieve himself as close to bedtime as possible. The later you take him out, the more likely you'll be able to get a few hours of sleep before he needs to go out again. Remember, puppies will need to go out every few hours, so be prepared to go out a few times per night. The general rule of thumb with puppies is that they can go one hour for every month of their age before needing another bathroom break. If you've brought home an eight-week-old puppy, you can assume that you will need to take him out every two hours or so. If you've brought home an adult Vizsla, he may be able to hold it all night, but don't count on it until you get to know him better. You may want to take

TIPS FOR THE FIRST WEEK HOME

By: Linda Maus – MausHaus Vizslas

Your new puppy has just left the only home he has ever known, his breeder, mother, and littermates. He has always had someone to play with and another warm puppy to lie next to. While he is excited to be with his new family, he is missing his previous life. He is not sure if he is staying with you; it is a confusing and frightening time for a puppy. I suggest you prepare an enclosed area/bedding just for puppy. Include a blanket, toys, and water bowl. Some breeders will send puppy home with a scented litter blanket; that is very comforting.

During the busy daytime when puppy is playing and watching his surroundings, he will be active and happy. Once the activity quiets down at bedtime is when puppy begins to feel lonely. I suggest that you set up a nightly routine leading up to bedtime. Dogs are creatures of habit, so it is best to go for the last evening walk at a consistent time. You may want to place a crate at your bedside so puppy doesn't feel alone. It should be easy for you to reach down with your hand and reassure him if he wakes during the night.

Puppies, like babies, cry or bark for various reasons. Vizslas will cry if they are lonely or want attention, as they are very people oriented. If puppy fusses a lot during the night, it may be that he needs to go for a quick walk. Don't have puppy think it is play time by talking to him or turning on the light. Make the walk all about going potty, and promptly return him to his crate. To discourage overnight potty breaks, I recommend puppy does not have full access to the water bowl after 8 p.m. Allow a few sips as needed, but don't allow him to guzzle a whole bowl, which is just setting him up for failure.

Photo Courtesy
of Jodi Shea

him out once or twice per night just to be sure or until you are confident in his housetraining.

Regardless of your Vizsla's age, be prepared for whining or crying during the night. It may take a few nights before you begin to understand the difference between his requests for a bathroom break and his demands for attention. If you've taken your Vizsla outside in the last hour or so, you can safely assume that his cries are for attention, but if it's been several hours or more, you need to take him out.

If your Vizsla is simply demanding attention, you need to ignore him as best as you can. At this stage, yelling or telling him no won't help much as he won't understand why you're upset. In many cases, even corrections will be seen as attention, and your dog may respond with more noise. It can be difficult to ignore a crying puppy, but responding will only encourage him, so do not let him out if you believe your Vizsla is asking for attention. Wait for him to quiet down so that he can be rewarded for being quiet rather than for throwing a tantrum. Be sure to take notice of how frequently you take your Vizsla outside during the first night. This will help you get an idea of where he's at in his housetraining so that you can develop a regular nightly schedule to adhere to.

CHAPTER 7
The First Few Weeks

> "
>
> *I recommend for the person who will be the primary care taker to take the first few days off of work. Vizslas are family dogs, but they also definitely belong to one person in the family. The biggest thing is patience with a calm, relaxed demeanor. One thing about Vizslas is that they want to make you happy. So once they figure out what it is that makes you happy, they will do it.*
>
> LISA WEST
> *Red Sky Kennel*
>
> "

Standing by Your Expectations

The first few weeks with your Vizsla are bound to be both exciting and stressful. However, it's crucial that you try to be as realistic about your expectations as possible. Vizslas are smart and adaptable dogs, but you must remember that your dog's entire life has been uprooted, and he's now living with strangers in an unfamiliar house, so you need to be patient and keep your expectations low. Additionally, you need to realize that your dog is a reflection of your training and commitment, so the more you are able to focus on teaching your Vizsla the rules of the house, the more quickly he's going to adapt to your family's lifestyle. If you plan on holding a single 20-minute training session each week, you're not going to see the same results as you would if you held shorter daily training sessions. When you train or enforce rules infrequently, you and your new dog are going to get frustrated since you'll likely spend more time reviewing what he knows than actually teaching him something new. That type of repetition will result in a frustrated dog that doesn't understand your expectations of him. As time goes on, he may also become increasingly less interested in participating in training sessions if it only ends in frustration.

This is not to say that you need to spend 24 hours per day focusing on your Vizsla's training. Remember, he's under a lot of stress at this time and may need plenty of free time to decompress, but you need to keep your expectations fairly low until he settles into his new life. During the first few weeks with your Vizsla, if the only things you accomplish are a basic understanding of your household rules, you should consider that a success. Vizslas are sensitive dogs and may not respond well to the intense pressure of a strenuous training program in a new environment, so work at a pace that is comfortable for

HELPFUL TIP
Velcro Vizslas

Vizslas are excellent companion dogs, so much so that they've earned the nickname "Velcro Vizslas." Still, this attachment to their humans can become troublesome if your Vizsla begins showing signs of separation anxiety. Early socialization is the key to many canine behavioral issues, and separation anxiety is no different. From an early age, practice leaving your dog in his crate or enclosure while leaving the house for increasingly longer periods of time. Put your dog in his safe space a few minutes before leaving, then leave without considerable fanfare. Vizslas need lots of exercise, so make sure your dog is also getting plenty of exercise and mental stimulation during the day since boredom can mimic separation anxiety.

you and your dog and try to keep your training sessions as fun as possible. By keeping your training sessions short and exciting, your Vizsla will be more engaged and interested in learning. This will also serve to minimize or eliminate any frustration or resentment that may develop with inconsistent or intense training.

Establishing Household Rules

> *A great thing to do is to set boundaries for your puppy. Take him around your house the first few days, showing him where he can go and keeping him out of the areas he isn't allowed to go. You really don't want a puppy going everywhere in your house when he first gets there...he will think he can go anywhere he wants.*
>
> **KATIE ALEXANDER**
> *Minnie Ridge Vizslas*

During the first few weeks at home with your new Vizsla, you'll have the opportunity to introduce him to the rules of your household. However, these rules must be enforced consistently, so it's crucial that all members of your family are on the same page. If you've discussed the rules before picking up your Vizsla, then you're ready to begin once you get home. However, if you haven't yet had this discussion with your family or thought about what rules you'd like to establish, now is the time to do so.

Photo Courtesy
of Robyn Glynn

*Photo Courtesy
of Van der Zwalmen Sandrine*

One of the most important rules that every Vizsla should know is to politely go through doorways. If you've adopted a puppy, it may not seem like a big deal if he pushes his way through the doorway, but it will become a problem as he gets larger and stronger, especially if you have children or seniors in your home or that visit frequently. A small child or elderly person could become seriously injured if they are knocked over by an overexuberant Vizsla on their way out the door.

It can be helpful to teach your Vizsla to sit before working on door manners, so refer to Chapter 12 if you aren't familiar with teaching this command. Each time you go through a doorway, especially when going outside, ask your Vizsla to sit politely before you open the door. Encourage him to make eye contact with you to ensure that he's listening. The first few times you try this, he will likely get excited and try to shove his way out, especially if you're going outside. Once your Vizsla is sitting quietly and is focused on you, you can release him using your verbal marker of choice, such as "OK." If he tries to leave his position before you release him, simply return him to a sitting position and try again. With practice, he'll understand that he's not allowed to go through the doorway until permitted.

Another crucial rule to teach your Vizsla is to move out of the way when asked. This is important in preventing your new dog from developing resource guarding behaviors. If you ask your Vizsla to move out of the middle of the hallway or off the furniture and he refuses, you're allowing him to be the one in charge. With time, this could lead to him expressing aggressive behavior when asked to move out of the way.

There are several ways to teach your dog to move when asked, and the method of choice will depend on your dog. If you've brought home a puppy, it's likely that he doesn't know enough to say no to you, but an adult dog may already have opinions about moving when asked, and he may react differently. One method involves having your Vizsla wear a "drag line" or short leash while relaxing around the house. The drag line should not be left on if the dog is unsupervised.

Drag lines are particularly useful for dogs that react negatively if their collars are grabbed. If your dog does not move when asked, you can reinforce your request by grabbing the drag line and encouraging him to move with gentle leash pressure. You can also lure him out of the way with treats if you'd like. If you're asking him to get off the furniture, wait until all four paws are on the ground before rewarding. You may also attempt to gently push your dog off the furniture with your hands, but some dogs may react negatively to this method, so use it with caution. Remember to verbally praise your Vizsla once he moves out of the way or all four feet are on the floor.

Puppy Problems

> 66
>
> *I give my Vizsla puppies lots of toys of all kinds to keep them active. The more safe things they have to chew on, the better. My pups do not chew on anything in the house that I do not want them to, and I attribute this to having a lot of safe stuff for them to chew. I also tell everyone when they get their pup that even though the toys are FOR the dog, nothing BELONGS to it. You want to make sure that resource guarding does not set in, so practice taking things away from your pup in the beginning.*
>
> **NANCY ANDERSON**
> *Anderson Vizslas*
>
> 99

*Photo Courtesy
of Lee and Jessica Barwick*

DEVELOPING A SOFT MOUTH

By: Stephen J Shlyen - Rheingold Vizslas

Vizslas are very curious, have a wonderful nose and a lot of drive, but they are also a mouthy breed. Don't confuse "mouthiness" with biting. Vizslas are bred to carry birds with a soft mouth. Do not tug your dog; this trains for a hard mouth. You may, when the dog is young, get down on the floor and hold a toy in your mouth and share with your dog. Never use your hand to tug. Vizslas are retrievers as well as pointers, so you will work with your Vizsla to retrieve those items you don't want him to chew. He will learn from your actions—you can have this; you can't have that. When a pup brings you your sock or underwear or one of those baby toys, take it gently from his mouth (use your hands softly to open his mouth), say thank you, give praise, but don't give it back to him. Say, "Good dog." When he brings you something you would let him have—a soft dog toy, for instance—also take it gently, then give it back to him, praise, take it again maybe, give back, praise...and off he goes, scampering away.

Although every Vizsla owner hopes that the first few weeks with their puppy go well, there will inevitably be a few problems to deal with. The most common puppy problems are easily corrected, but corrections must be consistent in order for the dog to understand what is inappropriate. It is far easier to prevent bad habits from developing than it is to correct them, so consistency is key. With most puppies, it comes down to proper supervision and management. Many bad habits are self-rewarding, so it's crucial that you manage your Vizsla puppy's environment in a way that does not allow him the opportunities to make bad choices.

One of the most common complaints from puppy owners is chewing. Unfortunately, chewing is unavoidable as it's a naturally occurring behavior of puppies of all breeds. Puppies tend to explore the world around them with their mouths, but chewing tends to intensify during the teething period between four and six months of age. As your Vizsla's adult teeth replace his puppy teeth, the pain and discomfort of the process may prompt him to chew more in an attempt to soothe his aching mouth. It's especially important to avoid giving your puppy the opportunity to chew inappropriate items during this period of time. Do not leave your puppy loose in the house without constant supervision, or you will certainly come home to chewed-up shoes, furniture, or personal belongings. To discourage inappropriate chewing, give him options such as chew toys or edible chews, and be sure to supervise him. There are also a variety of toys on the market that are designed to be frozen prior to chewing to help ease the discomfort of teething.

Another common puppy problem is digging. Digging can be a problem for puppies both in indoor spaces as well as outside. Leaving your Vizsla unsupervised in any area outside of his crate or playpen is asking for trouble. Many Vizslas begin digging as a way to entertain themselves when left alone for long periods of time. They may dig at furniture, carpet, or rugs indoors or in your garden or yard outside. Some puppies may also dig at potted plants if they are placed where the puppy can reach.

Digging can not only make a mess and cause expensive damage to your home, but your Vizsla could be at risk of damaging his paws or nails or ingesting rocks, sticks, dirt, or pieces of flooring or furniture. If your puppy is left unsupervised for long enough, he may also dig a large enough hole to crawl under your fence and escape. Digging can be a difficult habit to break once it starts, so it's important that you discourage your Vizsla from doing so from the very beginning. Typically, digging is easily interrupted with a sharp "No!" or a loud clap or stomp. Once your dog's attention is on you and not on whatever he was digging at, you can redirect him to more appropriate play, such as with a toy or a game of chase.

Vizslas are generally not particularly vocal dogs, but excessive barking can become a problem if the dog is not taught to be quiet. Most owners allow and even encourage a few warning barks when their Vizsla notices something unusual such as a visitor at the door, but any more than that should be considered a nuisance. If left alone for long periods, some dogs may also resort to barking to entertain themselves or express their frustration.

To discourage excessive barking, you must first teach your Vizsla the value of silence. If he begins barking excessively, you can again use a "No!" or a clap or stomp to interrupt his behavior. Once he is quiet, you can reward him with a treat and plenty of praise. Your Vizsla will soon learn that being quiet will get him a tasty treat or attention, while barking will result in an unpleasant noise from you. Eventually, you can add a quiet command, but it's important that your dog understand the desired behavior before you attach a word to it.

Photo Courtesy
of The Neesen Family

Adult Dog Problems

If you have adopted an adult Vizsla, it's possible that you won't have any problem behaviors to deal with in your first few weeks with your new companion. However, it's more likely that you'll have a few bumps in the road in terms of bad habits. Chewing is not limited to puppies, especially if it was not discouraged in your dog's previous home. As with puppies, the best way to deal with a problem chewer is to provide him with plenty of appropriate items to chew. With adult dogs, chewing is often a symptom of boredom, so it's important that you make sure your Vizsla is getting enough mental and physical stimulation each day.

Marking indoors can also be a common problem encountered by owners of adult Vizslas. Male dogs frequently lift their leg to urinate on items such as bushes or trees to mark their territory. Unless a dog has been taught otherwise, he may generalize the behavior and attempt to mark indoors. This bad habit should be dealt with the same way as you would with an untrained puppy.

Do not give your adult Vizsla the opportunity to mark inside your home. If you are unable to supervise him closely, he needs to remain in his crate, playpen, or designated area. You may also consider having him wear a long leash that can be attached to you to make sure that he's close enough to correct if he does attempt to mark. You may also have your Vizsla wear a belly band, which is simply a strip of absorbent fabric that can be worn around the waist. That way, when the dog tries to mark, the urine is absorbed into the belly band and will not stain your walls, floor, or furniture. If your Vizsla does manage to mark in your home, make sure to clean it up with an enzymatic cleaner that will eliminate the odor and stain while also reducing the dog's urge to go in the same place.

Running away is another common problem with adult Vizslas, but like many other problems, it can be solved with proper management. Your first step should be to eliminate the possibility of your dog running away from you. Do not allow him to be off-leash outside or indoors when he is out of his crate. Have him wear a long line outside and a drag line indoors. That way, you can grab the leash and get control of him should he attempt to run away. Second, you need to teach him a solid recall. For more information on this process, consult Chapter 12. It can be helpful to carry a small bag or pocketful of treats with you while at home with your dog. This way, you can reward him when he comes to you, and he'll learn the value of coming when called.

Leaving Your Dog Home Alone

> *While it is important to have someone home most of the time, it's important to also make sure that the Vizsla has alone time in its crate. Occasionally it's okay to go out and enjoy a dinner or a movie. Some time away from your dog will foster more independence. But make sure to keep the length brief so your dog understands that you are only gone for a short amount of time.*
>
> **SUSAN NAKAMURA**
> *Suzu Vizslas LLC*

There are times when your Vizsla will need to be left alone. Vizslas tend to bond closely with their owners and are prone to developing separation anxiety, so it's important to build a foundation for your dog prior to leaving him alone for long periods of time. The most important aspect is to be as calm as possible when entering or leaving your home. Even if you've just gone out to get the mail, you need to act the same way as if you were leaving for a full day of work. Do not make a big deal about leaving, and do not acknowledge your dog's excitement. When you come back inside, ignore your dog completely for several minutes until he's calmed down. Take your time taking off your shoes and putting your stuff away. Once your Vizsla has calmed down, you can quietly say hello to him without riling him up again.

If your Vizsla has developed separation anxiety in his previous home, or you've spent a significant amount of time home with him during his first few weeks or months, you'll need to convince him that being home alone isn't a big deal. To practice, you can go through your daily routine of putting on shoes and a jacket, grabbing your keys or purse, and walking out the door. Wait a few seconds and come back inside and put everything away just as you would when coming home from work or school. Give your dog several minutes to calm down before acknowledging him. Repeat the process and stay outside for longer as your dog begins to understand that he's not being abandoned. If your Vizsla can be trusted, you may also consider leaving him with a delicious chew or his favorite toy to play with while you're gone to keep him busy.

If your Vizsla is your only pet, you may also want to consider getting him a companion. Dogs are pack animals and tend to do best with a buddy of the same species, but many dogs are happy to have a feline friend as well. It's important to consider your Vizsla's personality and preferences and whether you're willing and able to keep up with the care of another animal before you commit to a second pet. If you're ready for the commitment of another animal, your Vizsla may be happier to be left alone at home if he's not truly alone. If you need help introducing your Vizsla to other pets, turn to Chapter 11: The Multi-pet Household.

Training Classes

> *I encourage all puppy owners to attend puppy kindergarten for basic instruction and socialization. A good six week/six-hour course is meant to train YOU how to train your dog. Some new owners are under the impression that at the end of six weeks their dogs will be 'trained.' Well, probably not. It really depends on how much consistent training you do at home every day that will make the difference. To achieve success, you must be patient, consistent, timely, and work by the theory of positive reinforcement.*
>
> **LINDA MAUS**
> *MausHaus Vizslas*

Unless you are an experienced dog trainer, you may want to consider signing your Vizsla up for training classes. Training classes are a great way to get professional advice not only on basic obedience training but household manners and housetraining as well. Training classes are also an ideal opportunity to socialize your Vizsla in a controlled environment. Whether you have a puppy or an adult dog, a class can help you teach your dog important skills such as sitting, staying, and recalling.

If you're signing your Vizsla puppy up for a training class, it's important to be aware that most training facilities have age limitations for puppies. You probably won't be able to take your Vizsla to class until he is at least 16 weeks of age. By that age, he will be fully vaccinated, and it will be safe for him to be around strange dogs in a new environment. Puppies younger than 16 weeks cannot be fully vaccinated, and their delicate immune systems make them more susceptible to infection by disease or parasites. Prior to class or on your first day, you may be required to provide proof of vaccinations or flea and tick prevention.

Adult dogs are not permitted to attend puppy classes, but your Vizsla will be able to attend a beginner obedience course designed for older puppies or adult dogs. These classes may be offered by training facilities, pet stores, or shelters. Individual trainers can also be found to offer you private lessons in your home or at a local park or training facility. If your Vizsla has any behavioral problems, private lessons may be needed before you can attend a group class. Training varies in price according to location and trainer experience, but private lessons tend to be more expensive than group lessons.

> 66
>
> *Vizslas cannot take harsh training. Usually a sharp 'no' or 'eth' (sounds like a growl) is enough to stop a pup. I like to have all my people go to training classes and learn how to train the pups themselves. Calling in a trainer for special problems is okay, but dogs should be able to learn by taking them to an organized training class usually held by an obedience club. Most Vizslas also respond well to positive training with treats or a clicker. I tell my people when making a correction to make it only to the degree they get the response they are looking for.*
>
> **NANCY ANDERSON**
> *Anderson Vizslas*
>
> 99

Taking It Slow

Your first few weeks with your Vizsla will be exciting and stressful. You'll experience a range of emotions from frustration to utter joy. Despite the ups and downs of the time you spend getting to know your new companion, it's important to remain patient no matter the challenge you're facing. Try to keep your expectations low and stay as positive and upbeat as possible. This is a stressful period for both you and your dog, so don't let your negative emotions get the better of you.

While it may be tempting to begin a strenuous training regimen the moment you bring your new Vizsla home, remember to take it slow to avoid overwhelming him. Training sessions should be short and sweet, and don't forget to quit before your Vizsla begins to lose focus. If he seems to struggle with a certain concept, return to something more familiar so that you can end on a positive note. You can always try the more challenging task at a later time when you're both rested and better able to focus. Positivity is essential during this initial training period, so try not to overwhelm your Vizsla with too much too quickly.

Remember, the first few weeks should be about building your relationship, as well as introducing basic concepts. Frustration will hinder the development of your relationship and make your Vizsla less excited about engaging with you, so try to keep your training as positive as possible.

Photo Courtesy of Cliff Tredway

CHAPTER 8
Health and Wellness

Choosing a Veterinarian

Unless your Vizsla is your first pet, you may already have a preferred veterinarian in your area. If not, you'll need to find one, so be prepared for a bit of research. Finding the right veterinarian is a bit like finding the

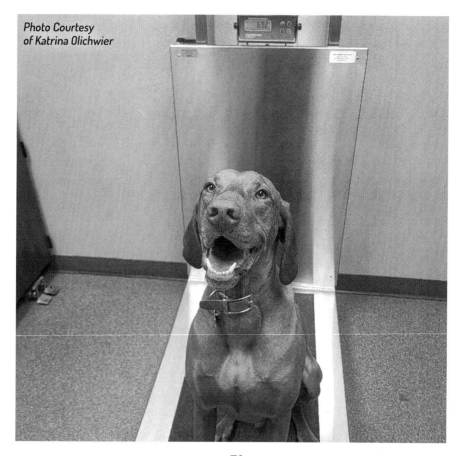

Photo Courtesy of Katrina Olichwier

right doctor for yourself. It may take some time to find the right fit, but once you do, you know your Vizsla will receive the right medical care.

If you've purchased your Vizsla from a local breeder or shelter, you may be able to ask them for a recommendation. Some rescue organizations take the dogs in their care to a local veterinarian for care, while others may have an in-house vet, so they may or may not be able to recommend a clinic. Breeders will have an ongoing relationship with a veterinarian, so if you live near the breeder, he or she will probably be able to give you guidance. Plus, that vet will have already been caring for your Vizsla since he was born, and you'll know that the vet will be familiar with the breed.

HELPFUL TIP
Epilepsy Research Initiative

In 2014, the University of Minnesota College of Veterinary Medicine began conducting phase 3 of a study into genetic markers for epilepsy in Vizslas and Australian Shepherds. Finding a genetic marker for this disease would allow for more informed breeding of these dogs. Epilepsy is frequently an inherited disease that presents itself between six months and three years. As of 2021, research is still ongoing.

Another great resource to consult is any dog-owning friends or family members, especially if they own Vizslas or similar breeds. If you're working with a local trainer or even a groomer, he or she may also be able to provide you with a recommendation. Fellow students in your training classes may also have a veterinarian that they can suggest to you. The more dog people you surround yourself with, the more opinions you'll be able to source.

If you need further help finding a veterinarian, consider browsing the directory on the American Veterinary Medical Association (AVMA) website. If you would prefer a more holistic approach to your Vizsla's care, the American Holistic Veterinary Medical Association (AHVMA) has a list on its website that can be searched by species and treatment type.

It's also important to consider your schedule when searching for a veterinarian. If you work during the week and would prefer weekend appointments for routine care, you should find a vet with availability on Saturdays and possibly Sundays. Some clinics are only open Monday through Friday, while others may be open 24 hours per day. Clinics that are open around the clock are ideal for after-hours emergency care should your Vizsla get sick or injured during the evening or weekend. Some clinics will also offer low-cost vaccine or spay and neuter events, which is helpful if you're caring for your Vizsla on a tight budget.

What to Expect During the First Visit

Your Vizsla's first appointment with the veterinarian is an opportunity for him to get to know his medical providers and vice versa. Make sure you show up to your appointment on time so that your veterinary team has plenty of time to work with your Vizsla, especially if he's nervous about new situations. If you have any of your dog's medical records, such as previous vaccinations, be sure to bring them along. During this first visit, it's important for you to remain calm so that your Vizsla understands that there's nothing to worry about.

If your Vizsla puppy is younger than 16 weeks of age, it's unlikely that he is fully vaccinated, so his first veterinary visit will be to update his vaccine history. However, until he is fully vaccinated, you need to be careful about exposing him to the outside world. Puppies have delicate immune systems, and even if he's had one or two boosters already, your Vizsla may still contract serious illnesses such as distemper or parvovirus. If you are able to carry your puppy, it's recommended to do so in areas that are visited by many dogs, such as the waiting room of the vet clinic.

The appointment will likely begin with the veterinary technician, who will greet your dog and weigh him. He or she will then record your Vizsla's heart rate, respiration, and body temperature. You may be asked questions about your dog's diet and any concerns you may have. After the vet tech has finished gathering information, you'll probably see the veterinarian next, who will perform a physical examination from nose to tail. Depending on your Vizsla's age and medical history, he may receive a booster vaccine and dewormer. Other tests or procedures may also be performed, depending on your dog's overall health.

Your veterinarian may also check your Vizsla for internal parasites by performing a fecal exam. This involves the collection of a fecal sample, which is then observed under a microscope, where any worms, eggs, larvae, or protozoa may be seen. Once the parasite has been identified, the correct medication can be prescribed. Most internal parasites are easily treated with a few doses of oral or injectable medication.

A common internal parasite that will not be identified in a fecal exam is heartworm. This parasite lives in the bloodstream and is spread by mosquitos. Particularly heavy parasite loads can be fatal, so routine testing and treatment are important, especially if you live in areas where heartworm is common. To test for heartworm, your veterinarian will collect a blood sample. Treatment for heartworm can take several months, and physical activity must be limited, but most dogs recover without any problems. For more information on internal parasites, see Chapter 16: Basic Health Care.

At your Vizsla's first vet visit, your veterinarian may bring up the topic of spaying or neutering if your dog has not yet been altered. Some vets

Photo Courtesy of Isabella Engle

recommend spaying or neutering at around six months of age, but recent advances in research have prompted many vets to encourage owners to wait until their dogs are more physically mature before removing their hormone-producing organs. Your dog's overall health and your goals for your dog will also affect when this surgery is performed, if at all. For example, dogs cannot compete in conformation after being spayed or neutered, so if you intend to show your dog, you may want to mention this to your vet.

If you're uncertain about the surgery but do not feel comfortable managing an intact dog, you might consider asking your vet about alternatives such as a vasectomy or ovary-sparing spay, which will allow your Vizsla to keep necessary hormones but will not allow him to reproduce. Again, more information on these procedures can be found in Chapter 16. If budget is a concern, you may want to ask about the cost for these procedures so you can begin saving up.

Tail Docking

Tail docking is a somewhat controversial procedure that is illegal in much of the world. In North America, it is common to dock the tails of Vizslas. According to the breed standard, one-third of the tail is typically docked, leaving two-thirds of the tail intact. This is not required for show dogs, but it is common practice in countries where it is legal.

Tails are generally docked when puppies are just a few days old and may be removed by an experienced breeder or a licensed veterinarian. Tail docking is typically performed to minimize the risk of injury in the field, but many Vizslas hunt successfully for years without injury. If you have strong opinions on docking, you may want to consider that when researching breeders. Some breeders do not dock tails, while others adhere to common breed practice.

Docked tails can be at risk of developing neuroma, also known as a nerve tumor, which can be incredibly painful. Dogs with neuroma are typically very sensitive about their rear ends. Opponents of docking also claim that docking can interfere with a dog's ability to communicate with other dogs since tails are an important aspect of canine body language. However, few studies have been done to prove or disprove this information. Whether or not you wish to have a Vizsla with a docked tail is a personal choice, but it's important to be aware of the risks of any cosmetic procedure. However, unless you've specifically sought out a breeder that does not dock tails, you likely won't have to worry about the procedure since it will have been done shortly after your Vizsla's birth.

Photo Courtesy of Emma Berry

Dangerous Foods

Nearly every dog owner is aware of common dangerous foods like chocolate, caffeine, and alcohol, but there are many other lesser-known human foods that are toxic to our canine companions. One of the most dangerous ingredients found in a wide variety of human foods is an artificial sweetener called xylitol. It's found in everything from sugar-free candy and gum to peanut butter and pudding. It's even used in toothpaste, lozenges, and gummy vitamins. When ingested by a dog, xylitol causes a dramatic drop in blood sugar within 10 to 60 minutes. Left untreated, hypoglycemia can be fatal. Higher doses of xylitol can also cause liver failure and seizures.

Other toxic foods include onions and garlic, which contain a substance called N-propyl disulfide. This substance causes damage to the red blood cells and can be fatal in large doses. Grapes and raisins are also toxic and can lead to kidney failure. The exact substance in these foods responsible for the reaction has yet to be identified. If you believe your Vizsla has eaten something toxic, seek veterinary attention immediately. The sooner your dog can get treatment, the more likely he is to survive.

Even if a food is not toxic, it can cause serious health problems in large doses. High-fat foods like peanut butter and cheese should only be fed in moderation. In addition to contributing to obesity, fatty foods put excess strain on your Vizsla's endocrine system and can cause pancreatitis. Overly salty foods like bacon, popcorn, or ham should also be fed in moderation, if at all. Some dogs may also be sensitive to dairy foods containing lactose, such as yogurt and cottage cheese. Additionally, high-sugar foods like ice cream, candy, and cookies should not be fed as they can cause serious digestive upset.

Common Health Problems in Vizslas

In general, Vizslas are a healthy breed with few common issues. This is especially true if you purchase a dog from a reputable breeder who performs all health tests recommended by the national breed club. Even if you have a Vizsla from a healthy background, it is important to be aware of the health conditions that are prevalent in the breed. Though health testing reduces the likelihood of a dog developing any genetic diseases in the future, it does not completely eliminate the possibility. If your Vizsla does test positive for any of these common health problems, it's important to notify your breeder as he or she will want to know so that any decisions can be made about repeating that breeding in the future.

Hip and Elbow Dysplasia

Although environmental and dietary factors can contribute to hip and elbow dysplasia, it is primarily a genetic condition. If a dysplastic dog is bred, its offspring are at a far higher risk of developing dysplasia than if both parents had been cleared for the condition. Of course, this does not mean that the puppy is guaranteed not to develop hip or elbow dysplasia, but its chances are certainly better.

Photo Courtesy of Sarah Rizkallah

Both hip and elbow dysplasia are a result of a deformity in the joint. Both hip and elbow dysplasia encompass several specific conditions, including but not limited to osteochondrosis (OCD), joint incongruity, and cartilage anomaly. These conditions simply describe the specific type of joint deformity. Although some dogs may show no symptoms, others will be lame on the affected limb or show a loss of muscle mass. If both front and hind limbs are affected, it can be more difficult to detect lameness, so x-rays are required for a formal diagnosis. Treatment of the condition will depend on the severity of the issue as well as the specific joint deformity, but surgery is generally recommended. The earlier that the condition is detected and addressed, the better the outcome. Hip and elbow dysplasia are progressive diseases, so the dog's condition will get worse over time.

Eye Problems

Vizslas are at risk of developing a variety of eye problems, including glaucoma, cataracts, distichiasis, and entropion. As with humans, canine glaucoma is an increase in eye pressure that can result in pain, redness, and a loss of vision. Glaucoma can have genetic factors but may also be caused by injury or other diseases such as uveitis or anterior dislocation of the lens. Common symptoms include eye pain, sensitivity around the head or face, watery discharge, lethargy, or swelling or bulging of the eye. Treatment must be prescribed quickly to prevent a loss of vision.

Canine cataracts are caused by a cloudy or opaque lens in the eye. It is generally a genetic condition but may also be caused by injuries or diseases such as diabetes. However, cataracts may also be age-related or occur spontaneously. Without treatment, cataracts can progress to a complete loss of vision. Surgery is generally the only course of treatment, but thankfully cataracts are not painful.

Distichiasis is a common eye condition where extra eyelashes are produced from an abnormal location or grow at an unusual angle. This can result in irritation to the eye by the eyelashes. Distichiasis is considered a genetic disorder, and symptoms include eye discharge, pain, and inflammation. If left untreated, the condition can result in an ulcerated cornea. Mild cases may not require treatment, but more severe cases will require medication or surgery.

Entropion is an ocular condition where the dog's eyelids roll inward, causing the eyelashes or other hair to rub and irritate the eyeball. It can affect the upper or lower eyelids and may be seen in one or both eyes. Symptoms include squinting, excessive tearing, redness, and discharge. Entropion is considered to be a hereditary disorder, though the exact genetic cause is unknown. Surgery is typically required to resolve the issue.

Heart Problems

Vizslas are also prone to heart issues, with the most common condition being a heart murmur. Though some heart murmurs can be caused by heart disease, others may be caused by issues such as heartworms or anemia. Heart murmurs are graded by intensity, with a Grade I murmur being soft or intermittent, while a Grade VI is intense enough to be felt by placing a hand on the dog's chest. Some dogs will not experience any issues with their hearts, particularly if the murmur is of a lower grade. However, others may display symptoms such as poor appetite, weight loss, breathing problems, poor exercise tolerance, coughing, or fainting. The dog's prognosis and whether medication is required for treatment will depend on the severity as well as the dog's symptoms.

Autoimmune Thyroiditis

The most common cause of hypothyroidism in dogs is autoimmune thyroiditis. The age of onset varies, but most dogs begin to show symptoms around two to five years of age. Hypothyroidism is caused by a deficiency of a hormone called thyroxine. Symptoms include weight gain and obesity, as well as hair loss and skin problems. Annual testing of dogs over the age of four is recommended for breeding dogs to help breeders determine which dogs are at risk of developing autoimmune thyroiditis. Thankfully, treatment for hypothyroidism consists of a daily medication, which is typically quite inexpensive.

Sebaceous Adenitis

Another common condition found in Vizslas is sebaceous adenitis, which is an immune-mediated disorder that causes inflammation in the sebaceous glands in the dog's skin. The sebaceous glands are responsible for producing a substance to help keep the skin and coat soft and supple. The age of onset typically occurs between young adulthood and middle age. Symptoms include dull or brittle coat, patchy hair loss, skin scales or lesions, and scarring. Sebaceous adenitis can be diagnosed with a skin biopsy. Unfortunately, the disease is challenging to treat, and there is no definitive treatment plan, but various topical and oral medications may be prescribed.

Vizslas and Extreme Temperatures

Although Vizslas are hardy dogs that were bred to spend plenty of time outdoors, they can be sensitive to extreme temperatures. Generally, most Vizslas will handle heat better than cold, but it's important to make sure that your Vizsla is taken care of when spending time outside in extreme weather.

During heat waves, make sure your Vizsla has access to clean, fresh water at all times. If you plan on keeping your Vizsla outside during hot weather, such as in an outdoor kennel or run, you'll also need to make sure he has shelter. A doghouse or covered kennel area is ideal for protecting your dog from the elements. Don't forget that pavement and concrete can be hot enough to burn paws in hot weather. You can test the temperature of the concrete with your hand if you're unsure whether it's safe for your dog to touch. If you cannot keep your hand on the surface for very long, your dog will not be able to walk or stand there safely.

If you're simply exercising your Vizsla outdoors in the heat, keep a close eye on him to make sure that he can take a break with shade and water when needed. Excessive panting is typically the first sign of heatstroke, but also look out for drooling and reddened gums. Vomiting, diarrhea, confusion, and uncoordinated movements are also possible. In extreme cases, the dog may also collapse. If you believe your Vizsla is experiencing heatstroke, seek veterinary care immediately.

Photo Courtesy of Samantha M. D'Anna

Vizslas are particularly sensitive to cold weather due to their short, sleek coats and are not a breed that should be kept outside during the winter. They are not equipped to deal with extreme cold and must be allowed indoors to warm up. Although they can gain some tolerance with exposure to cold, many owners opt to keep their Vizslas warm with sweaters or jackets. These are particularly useful in ensuring your Vizsla gets enough exercise during frigid weather. Many different sizes and styles can be found on the market, but be sure that your dog's clothing does not limit his range of motion in any way. Depending on your dog and climate, you may also want to consider buying booties to protect your Vizsla's paws from ice and snow.

Remember, wetness can increase your Vizsla's risk of hypothermia in cold weather, so if the weather is wet and cold, keep your walks short or invest in a doggie jacket with better coverage. Signs of hypothermia in dogs include paleness of the gums and strong shivering. In severe cases, the dog may also be listless or lethargic. If immediate veterinary care is not provided, coma and heart failure are possible. If you believe your Vizsla is developing hypothermia, remove him from the cold immediately and seek veterinary care. You can wrap him in warm blankets and provide a warm water bottle or heating pad on your way to the vet. Dogs typically have a normal body temperature between 101°F and 102.5°F, so anything under 100°F is considered hypothermic.

CHAPTER 9
Housetraining

Different Options for Housetraining

> *Vizslas are a smart breed, and with this trick they will house-train quickly. Most house-training accidents occur when the owner is not in tune with the puppy's clues. Pacing, jumping, barking, hiding are some clues your puppy needs to go out immediately. Our home has many exterior doors, but I suggest being consistent and always using the same door to take your puppy out to potty. I hang a hunting bell from the doorknob, so when opened, it rings. When I see a puppy pacing near that door or sitting on the mat in front of that door, I know puppy needs to go out. As they get older, they instinctively know to nose the bell to reproduce the sound when they want the door opened.*
>
> **LINDA MAUS**
> *MausHaus Vizslas*

House-training can be a time-consuming challenge for any Vizsla owner, but with patience and consistency, it can be accomplished. Vizslas are intelligent dogs that enjoy pleasing their owners, so housetraining typically doesn't take as long as it might with other breeds. If you've brought home a puppy or untrained adult Vizsla, you're going to need to spend more time and focus on housetraining than if you've adopted an already trained adult. However, even if your Vizsla has already been housetrained, it's important to remember that the stress of moving into a new home can cause even the most well-behaved dog to make a mistake or two. Housetraining is always easiest when you know your options and have a plan to follow, so you'll need to decide which method works best for your family.

Photo Courtesy of Tracy Mucci

Traditional housetraining encourages a dog to relieve himself outside only. Some owners may choose to teach their Vizslas only to relieve themselves in a certain area of their yard or outdoor space, while others may decide that as long as it's outside, the exact location doesn't matter. It's important to note that some owners will rely on a dog's behavior to tell them when he needs to go out. Actions such as whining, pacing, or circling tend to be most common. Some owners will also teach their dogs to tell them when they want to go outside by having the dog touch a button or bell with his paw or nose. Neither method is better than the other, but you must spend some effort either learning your dog's behavior or teaching him new behaviors in order to avoid missing his cues.

While most owners choose not to use potty pads or patches with dogs as large as Vizslas, they can still be helpful tools in potty training, especially if you're working with a puppy. These tools allow your Vizsla to relieve himself indoors in a way that is not damaging to your home or his training regimen. They are especially helpful if you have to be out of the house for periods of time longer than your dog can hold it. When using potty pads and patches, most owners begin phasing them out as the dog develops the ability to hold his bladder and bowels for longer periods of time.

If you choose to rely on these products, you'll have more decisions ahead of you regarding the products themselves. Disposable puppy pads are the most common choice as they can simply be tossed in the trash once soiled. However, reusable puppy pads are less wasteful and are typically made of several layers of washable cloth materials. Potty patches are generally made of plastic and fake grass or turf. Beneath the turf is a waterproof tray that can be emptied and washed as necessary.

The First Few Weeks

> *Practice getting to know your pup's language! Be attentive. Watch him closely, as he will exhibit obvious signs. If he makes a mistake, do not punish him; direct him to where he should go and reward him. We suggest crate training, and we raise our pups in a large crate with the doors off. This way they get used to being in a crate by the time they go to their new families. It's okay to let them cry a little bit. They want to be near you. Remember, the crate is NOT to be used as a punishment. The crate should be a safe, happy place for dogs.*
>
> **PETER & LINDSAY SUGDEN**
> *Sunchaser Vizslas*

As previously stated, successful housetraining can only be accomplished with patience and consistency, so that should be your focus during the first few weeks. It can take several weeks for a Vizsla to settle into a new home, so don't expect much progress at first. The most important aspect of the first few weeks of housetraining is managing your Vizsla correctly. Do not allow him to roam the entire house unsupervised, or you are asking for a mess to clean up. The more unsupervised messes your dog is allowed to make, the more difficult housetraining will be. If you are unable to keep a close watch on your Vizsla, he needs to be in his crate or playpen.

It's also important to go easy on punishments during the first few weeks of housetraining. Vizslas are sensitive, and a harsh punishment will only damage your developing relationship and frighten or stress your new dog out. If you spot a mess but did not catch your Vizsla in the act, your only option is to clean it up and move on. You cannot correct a dog after the fact, so do not "rub his nose in it." Dogs do not have the ability to process past and current events the way we do, and your Vizsla will not make that connection.

If you do catch your Vizsla in the act of relieving himself indoors, do not scold or spank him. Physical punishments are inappropriate and harmful to your dog's mental health and training. He will not understand that you are hurting him because of his actions, and he may instead learn to only relieve himself if you aren't around.

When correcting your Vizsla's actions, you need to correct him quickly and move on. Do not dwell on his behavior or prolong the correction. A loud clap or stomp or "No!" will be adequate in interrupting the behavior without scaring the dog. Once you've interrupted him, immediately take him outside and allow him to finish. Once he finishes relieving himself in an appropriate area, reward him with praise, affection, and even treats. By quickly correcting and redirecting him, you're teaching your Vizsla that going potty indoors will be met with an unpleasant correction while going potty outside will be rewarded.

Photo Courtesy of Clayton Schrey

The Importance of Consistency

> " Be consistent and learn your puppy's signals. All family members should use the same terminology. In the beginning, take the puppy out to potty whenever the puppy wakes up, finishes eating, signals a desire to potty, and otherwise every 20 minutes. The fewer accidents you have in the house, the quicker learning actually goes. If the puppy pees in the house, screech and scoop the puppy up and finish outside. Be sure to give him lots of praise for going potty outside. "
>
> **CAROL B PHELPS**
> *Szizlin Vizslas, Reg.*

Although the repetition of this concept may seem unnecessary, consistency is crucial in housetraining any Vizsla. Inconsistent training will only result in your Vizsla misunderstanding your expectations. You may both become frustrated, which can be damaging to your relationship this early in the game. In order to ensure consistency, it's crucial that all members of your family are involved, especially if you've brought home a puppy. Each person should be aware of the supervision requirements and approximate bathroom break schedule your dog needs at his current age. You should also teach each member of the family how to correct the dog should they catch him in the act of relieving himself indoors, as well as how to properly clean up afterward. For young children, you may need to ask them to notify an adult rather than have them be directly involved in training or cleanup.

Positive Reinforcement

By rewarding your Vizsla every time he relieves himself in an appropriate area, you can convince him to repeat the behavior in the future through the use of treats and affection. Vizslas are intelligent dogs that learn quickly and love to please their humans, so it likely won't take long for your new companion to understand what you're asking of him.

Consistency is as important in rewards as it is in corrections, so in the beginning, you'll need to prepare to reward your Vizsla each and every time he goes to the bathroom outside. You can phase out the over-the-top rewards as he advances in his training, but those rewards are crucial in the early stages of housetraining. If you're using treats as rewards, it can be helpful to have a small bag of treats near your door so that you can easily grab them on your way out.

Another key aspect of positive reinforcement is the timing of rewards. The outdoors is an interesting place full of fascinating smells and space to run, so you need to factor that into your training equation. It's not uncommon for dogs, especially puppies, to get so wrapped up in outdoor play that they forget to go to the bathroom. The result is a puppy that immediately relieves himself once he comes back inside.

To resolve this issue, try to stay as calm and collected as possible when you first take your Vizsla outside. Do not let him off-leash or allow him to play. Walk him around until he's ready to relieve himself. As he's going, you can add a verbal command such as "go potty" so that you can eventually give him the command, and he'll understand what you want him to do. Use a calm and soothing voice to let him know that he's behaving correctly and save the excitement until he's done. Otherwise, you risk interrupting him, and he may finish in the house later. When he's finished, you can reward him with verbal praise, affection, treats, and freedom to play and explore the yard.

Photo Courtesy of Madison Rice

Cleaning Up

No matter how well trained your Vizsla is, you're guaranteed to have to clean up at least a few messes. It's important to have the right products on hand and use the right techniques to clean up to discourage your dog from returning to the same place in the future. Additionally, proper sanitization is essential for the health and safety of your entire family, both humans and animals.

When choosing a cleaning product, it's best to purchase one that has been designed specifically for use on pet messes. Pet-specific cleaning products are formulated to break down the elements responsible for lasting stains and odors. Some of the most effective cleaners on the market include unique ingredients such as enzymes to ensure that the area is thoroughly cleaned.

Photo Courtesy of Susie Phelan

The problem with cleaners not designed for pet messes is that they may clean up the stain and any odor detectible by you, but your dog has a much stronger sense of smell. A lasting odor may encourage him to return to that area to relieve himself. It's important to note that not all products work on all types of flooring, so you may need to buy more than one cleaning agent if you have different flooring throughout your home.

In addition to cleaning products, you should make sure you have other cleaning supplies on hand, such as cloth

FUN FACT
California Landslide

In 2020, a pair of filmmakers produced a short documentary film about the historic California landslide of May 2017 that buried the Pacific Coast Highway. The film, titled California Landslide: A Dog's True Story, is told from the perspective of the filmmakers' Vizsla named Anika. Filmmakers Dana Richardson and Sarah Zentz chose to tell the story of this natural disaster through their dog's eyes to add levity to an otherwise difficult topic and as a thank you to Anika for saving their lives. California Landslide was produced by Dana & Sarah Films.

towels or rags, paper towels, and scrub brushes. Again, the type of flooring in your home will dictate what supplies you should be using. Paper towels may work fine on hard surfaces such as linoleum, wood, or tile but will fall apart if used to scrub carpet. Cloth towels work well on all surfaces and can be washed after use rather than disposed of. Stiff-bristled brushes can be used to scrub hard flooring but may damage carpet.

There are also many small cleaning appliances on the market that you might consider investing in, such as carpet and steam cleaners. Portable carpet shampooing machines are generally the best way to thoroughly clean up a pet mess without professional help. For hard flooring, a steam cleaner is a popular choice as it also sanitizes the area as it cleans. However, steam can be damaging to some flooring, so it's important to know what type of product and appliance is best for your flooring.

Carpet tends to be the most difficult surface to clean, so if your home is carpeted, you need to make sure you're using the right products and techniques to ensure your home stays clean and sanitary. It's generally recommended to test any cleaning products in an inconspicuous area to ensure that they won't discolor or damage the carpet. If you need to scrub the carpet, it's best to use a cloth rag or a soft-bristled brush. Scrub lightly, though, as some carpet may begin unraveling if it is scrubbed too vigorously.

Playpens and Doggy Doors

During the early stages of housetraining, it's inadvisable to leave your Vizsla unsupervised outside of his crate. As he advances in his training, you can begin to give him a bit more freedom, even if you're not able to keep a close watch on him at all times. The first step beyond the crate is typically a playpen. Playpens will give your companion more space to play and stretch his legs, but not enough to get into too much trouble. As you introduce your Vizsla to the playpen, you can line the bottom with puppy pads. There are a

Photo Courtesy
of Lee and Jessica Barwick

few companies on the market that design puppy pads large enough for use with playpens. These pads are recommended as the edges will be beyond the boundaries of the playpen and won't be tempting for your puppy to pick up and chew.

It's important to note that playpens are not ideal for every dog. Some Vizslas may be well-behaved enough to be trusted without supervision, but others may knock over the walls or climb or jump over them to escape. You can train your Vizsla to respect the boundaries of his playpen, but you may not be able to leave him unsupervised at first.

If you have a safely fenced yard, you may also consider installing a doggy door to give your Vizsla more control over his own bathroom schedule. For many dogs, this can mean fewer accidents indoors as they won't need to rely on you to take them out. There is a range of different door styles available, including temporary doors that install in sliding patio doors and more permanent solutions that can be placed in walls or solid doors. Most doggie doors can be locked to prevent intruders from gaining access to your home while you're away. Some doors remain locked until approached by your dog, who wears a special tag on his collar that unlocks the door just for him. These doors are useful if you're worried about neighborhood strays or wildlife entering your home or if you have other pets that are not allowed outdoors, such as cats.

If you decide to install a doggy door, you'll need to make sure you buy the appropriate size for your Vizsla. Most doors have a rough guideline that you can use to estimate your Vizsla's preferred size, but if you have a puppy, it can be more difficult. Bigger doors can be harder for small puppies to manage, so you might consider using a temporary door of a smaller size before graduating to a larger permanent door as your Vizsla reaches adulthood.

When giving your Vizsla more freedom, you need to make sure he's ready for that responsibility. Introducing freedom too soon can significantly set back his housetraining. To further ensure success, make sure your Vizsla is getting enough physical and mental exercise each day. Otherwise, he may use his freedom to entertain himself in inappropriate and potentially destructive ways.

CHAPTER 10
Socialization

The Importance of Good Socialization

> *A Vizsla puppy can be very annoying to other dogs since they are extremely high energy. Therefore, supervision is a must. If the other dog gives signs that he is upset by the puppy, you must remove your Vizsla from the situation. One bite from another dog can cause lifelong issues.*
>
> **MARK AND PAM SPURGEON**
> *Crimson Sky Vizslas*

Socialization is a crucial aspect of raising a balanced and well-behaved Vizsla. A properly socialized Vizsla will be stable and predictable enough to take nearly anywhere. He will become more confident in himself, and you will both become more confident in your relationship. This is especially important if you plan to take your Vizsla with you on vacation or if you plan on showing or competing with him. Even if you occasionally take him to the local café for Sunday brunch, socialization will ensure that you have an enjoyable time together.

It's a common misunderstanding with novice dog owners that socialization need only be done as a puppy, and you'll have a well-behaved dog for the rest of his life. Unfortunately, this is not true, and you will need to socialize your Vizsla consistently throughout his life to maintain his confidence and his trust in you. Additionally, many people believe that socialization consists of meeting as many new dogs and people as possible within a certain time frame. Again, this is not correct and may result in an overwhelmed and possibly fearful dog.

Socialization is not just about meeting new people and dogs, but new sights, sounds, feelings, and smells as well, while also respecting a dog's comfort zone. Forcing your dog to be in uncomfortable situations will not socialize him, so if he ever seems anxious with a situation, it's best to back off. For instance, if your Vizsla is nervous around other dogs, do not take him to the dog park and hope for the best. Instead, approach the dog park from afar and only close that distance as your dog seems comfortable.

A well-socialized dog will be comfortable in a wide variety of situations, but it can be difficult to socialize a puppy that has not yet received all of his required vaccines. If it is not yet safe to take your Vizsla in public, you can socialize him at home by exposing him to new experiences like the sound of the hairdryer or blender. This breed can be sensitive, so it's important not to overwhelm them. Remember to praise and reward your Vizsla whenever he approaches a new situation with any amount of confidence.

Photo Courtesy
of Diana Szogi

Socializing Puppies

>
>
> *Do not make the mistake of overprotecting your dog too much from germs early on. It's better to socialize at an early age with other smaller dogs, active running dogs, and those who are playful and proven friendly. Remember that a healthy, playful puppy is well exercised, sleeps well, and often dreams while sleeping. You may see him running in his sleep, thinking about what fun he had and what tomorrow will bring.*
>
> **STEPHEN J SHLYEN**
> *Rheingold Vizslas*

If you've purchased your Vizsla from a reputable breeder, your puppy has probably already been started on socialization. Many reputable breeders use socialization programs such as Puppy Culture to prepare their litters for their new homes. Programs such as Puppy Culture are comprehensive, organized, and designed by professional trainers and behaviorists to set puppies up for socialization success. It's also a great way to begin working on the communication and relationship between puppy and human. Once your Vizsla comes home with you, it becomes your responsibility to continue the socialization process. Programs such as Puppy Culture are also designed to help puppies beyond the time they leave their mothers and littermates, so if you're interested in continuing a socialization program, ask your breeder for more information on their program of choice.

As previously mentioned, you will need to be careful about socializing your puppy prior to his being fully vaccinated. Puppies under the age of 16 weeks are vulnerable to dangerous pathogens, and care must be taken to keep them safe. However, there is still plenty of socialization that can be done at home, both indoors and outside. Be sure to have your puppy walk across many different surfaces, such as grass, concrete, soil, and wood. You can even expose him to small amounts of water in a splash pad or baby pool.

Handling should also be an important part of your at-home socialization work. This will help to prepare your Vizsla for future interactions with the vet and groomer. Be sure to get him used to you touching his feet and paws. If you plan on trimming your dog's nails at home, now is the time to start handling his feet. If you plan on brushing his teeth, you can also begin teaching him to tolerate that process too. Even if you don't plan on doing any of this at home, handling your Vizsla's paws, ears, and mouth will help him understand that it's nothing to be afraid of.

After your puppy has received his final vaccinations, including rabies, you can take him out into the world. Just be sure to go slowly to avoid overwhelming your Vizsla, especially during any fear periods. Start by exploring the areas around your home and neighborhood. You can also take him for short car rides. If you have friends with puppies or gentle older dogs, you can set up playdates. However, it's important to be careful which dogs you introduce your Vizsla to at this stage. Dog parks are unpredictable and chaotic environments that can permanently damage a young dog's confidence. Rather than expose your dog to potentially dangerous or scary situations, it's best to introduce him to other dogs in a more controlled environment. If you're interested in signing up for a puppy obedience class, you may be able to find one that allows some playtime in a safe and properly supervised environment.

The most important thing to consider when socializing your Vizsla puppy is to avoid overwhelming him. It's your responsibility to take care of his physical and mental well-being, so you need to ensure that he only has positive experiences. One bad experience can set a nervous puppy back several months, so it's crucial to proceed with caution. If your puppy begins acting nervous or fearful, consider backing away from the situation and either approaching from afar or trying again later. Once he begins to gain confidence, you can help him learn to work through that fear, but the first few months of socialization should be purely positive experiences if possible.

> 66
>
> *I recommend calling your local department stores, like Home Depot or Lowe's, to see if they will let you bring your puppy into their stores to help with socialization. Only let people pet the dog if all four paws are on the ground. This is also very helpful with teaching your puppy manners when greeting humans.*
>
> **KATIE ALEXANDER**
> *Minnie Ridge Vizslas*
>
> 99

Socializing Adult Dogs

> **"**
>
> *Socialize with stable, nonaggressive dogs. Dog parks are not good areas for Vizslas; females in particular are not happy to have strange dogs sniffing or overenthusiastically greeting them. Though some Vizslas are happy to play with other dogs, generally they are more interested in interacting with humans.*
>
> **WENDY RUSSELL**
> *Widdershins*
>
> **"**

Adopting an adult Vizsla is in many ways easier than adopting a puppy, but there are some unique challenges to socializing an adult dog. One of the greatest challenges you'll face is your dog's past socialization. If you've adopted your Vizsla from a reputable source, such as a breeder, you may have some knowledge about what his past home was like, but if you got him from a shelter, it might be more of a mystery. It's possible that he may have had traumatic experiences in his past that only come up during specific situations. Without knowing exactly what your Vizsla has been through in his past, it's difficult to predict how he will react to new situations. Some adult dogs may be confident in a wide range of situations, while others may surprise you by what they react to.

Since you may not know what kind of experiences your Vizsla has had in his life, it's often a good idea to approach his socialization as you would a puppy. Assume that he's going to be nervous and proceed with caution. It's best to approach any new situation from afar and only approach as quickly as your dog is comfortable with. Going slowly is especially important as you are just developing a relationship with your Vizsla, and you want to earn his trust. Thrusting him into overwhelming situations will not help him learn to trust you. Again, dog parks are not recommended, and you should consider only introducing him to dogs you know and trust.

If you are aware of past trauma in your Vizsla's life, proceed with extreme caution. For many fearful or reactive dogs, it can take months or even years to overcome past trauma and approach new situations with confidence. In these cases, it can be easy to become frustrated, but patience and consistency will pay off. If you have any doubts about your training ability or need help socializing your Vizsla, consider contacting a professional trainer or behaviorist.

Photo Courtesy
of The Neesen Family

Lifelong Socialization

> "
>
> *Take puppy out on a lead with many treats in your pocket. Where another dog is going by, pull off to the side, have the puppy focus on you, and treat, treat, treat. The puppy learns that others dogs are safe and good things happen around other dogs. Your puppy does not need to meet other dogs, and meetings can cause issues. Puppies are rude in the way they approach other dogs, and this can set the pup up for a bite of serious aggression.*
>
> JUDY HETKOWSKI
> *Boulder Vizslas*
> "

The more you socialize your Vizsla the easier the process will become. This will be due in part to the bond you're building between the two of you. As your dog learns to trust you, he will come to understand that you will never put him in a dangerous situation, even if it does make him a bit nervous. This is why it's so important to only expose him to situations with a positive outcome during the first few weeks or months together. As he develops trust in you, he'll be less likely to panic or shut down out of fear. Eventually, you may get to the point that you socialize your Vizsla without even thinking about it as you go about your daily adventures together.

Speaking of daily adventures, that is the primary benefit of a well-socialized Vizsla. The more you socialize your dog, the more comfortable he will be in new situations and the easier it will be to take him with you. You'll be able to compete at new venues or facilities, walk in unfamiliar neighborhoods, or take a road trip without worrying about how your Vizsla will handle it. Not only will these new experiences socialize your dog, but he'll get plenty of mental stimulation as he processes the new sights, sounds, and smells.

Dealing with High Prey Drives

As a breed developed for hunting, many Vizslas have a high prey drive. Though there are many Vizslas that are content to coexist with small prey animals, the majority prefer to give chase. This can make it challenging to fully trust your Vizsla around small animals such as cats, chickens, or pocket pets. For this reason, it's inadvisable to allow your Vizsla off-leash in unfenced areas until his recall is solid. More information on recall training can be found in Chapter 12.

If your Vizsla has a high prey drive, you will likely be unable to completely eliminate his urge to chase prey, but you can help him control it. Impulse training should begin as early as possible. If you've brought home a puppy, impulse training will be easier than with an adult dog who hasn't been taught these important skills. Regardless of your dog's age, you can begin working on your Vizsla's self-control as soon as you bring him home.

The most useful skill you can teach your Vizsla is to focus on you. This will help teach your dog the value of looking at you rather than prey animals. It can also be helpful with Vizslas that are reactive toward other dogs or animals. You can begin teaching this command in a quiet environment with few distractions, such as your home. Use your dog's favorite treats to get his attention and move the treat toward your face. When he looks at you, reward him. With practice, you can begin introducing a verbal command such as "watch me" or "focus." Eventually, he will make eye contact with you on command. At that point, you can ask for longer periods of eye contact and begin working in more distracting environments. If you find that you completely lose your Vizsla's focus, you may have progressed too quickly and need to return to a quieter environment or ask for a shorter duration of focus.

Photo Courtesy
of Katrina Olichwier

You may also need to accept that your Vizsla will never be able to be trusted around small animals. Some dogs may do fine when supervised but may take an opportunity to chase down an animal if you are not there to correct their behavior. If this is the case with your Vizsla, you will need to carefully manage his environment to ensure that he is not given the opportunity to injure or kill any small animals. Remember, even Vizslas trained to hunt are not allowed to dispatch the animals; they are only required to track them down and retrieve them.

Dealing with Fear

As you begin socializing your Vizsla, you will inevitably end up in a situation where he reacts out of fear. Being prepared will help you to handle your dog's fearful behavior and work through it. Though a responsible owner will try to avoid such situations, it's impossible to avoid them entirely. The important thing is to use it as a learning opportunity rather than let it become a setback.

FUN FACT

Matka the Bomb-Sniffing Vizsla

In 2016 a Vizsla joined the security team for the Minnesota capitol in Saint Paul. The canine security officer's name is Matka, and she was 18 months old when she joined the security detail. Her job is to sniff out explosives along with her human trooper companion, Kaj Meinhardt.

The first step in dealing with your Vizsla's fear is to recognize fearful body language and determine its severity. A mildly nervous dog may tuck his tail and flatten his ears. He may also pant, yawn, tremble, lick his lips, or avoid eye contact with those around him. At this stage, most dogs can be distracted or encouraged to overcome their fear. However, if the fear is not addressed or is encouraged, the dog's behavior may escalate to panic, and he may even attempt to escape. Panicked dogs also frequently lash out with aggression if they feel threatened, so addressing your dog's fear is essential to his safety and yours.

Photo Courtesy of Cynthia Hughes

In order to help your Vizsla work through his fear, you need to control your own emotions. If you allow yourself to express your nervous energy, your dog will certainly pick up on it, and his fear may escalate. You must behave in as calm and collected a manner as possible, even if you don't really feel that way. Leading by example will show your dog that there is nothing to be afraid of, and you have it all under control.

Though it may be tempting, it's important not to coddle or try to comfort your dog when he's afraid. He may interpret that as reassurance that his reaction is justified. However, you should not correct him either, as he may respond badly as a result of overstimulation. If your Vizsla is fearful, you should speak in a calm and level tone. If you can increase the distance between your dog and whatever he is afraid of, do so calmly and be sure to reward him once he starts to relax. This is also a great time to use your "focus" command to encourage him to pay attention to you rather than whatever is making him nervous.

Photo Courtesy of Clayton Schrey

Once your Vizsla has calmed down, you can reflect on the situation to determine whether you handled the situation appropriately or if there was something you could have done differently to calm your dog more quickly. Remember, these situations should be used as learning experiences for you and your Vizsla. If you realize that you're struggling to understand what went right or wrong during these events, or you don't think you can help your Vizsla work through his fear, consider seeking professional help. Fear can be a challenge for novice owners, and the sooner you consult a trainer or behaviorist, the sooner you and your Vizsla can tackle new situations with ease.

CHAPTER 11
The Multi-pet Household

Introducing a Puppy to Other Animals

One of the most stressful aspects of bringing home a new puppy is introducing him to your current pets. Generally, it's not the puppy you need to worry about so much as the older animals. Some Vizsla puppies may be nervous when meeting new animals, but others may be more enthusiastic. Even if your current pets are usually friendly or tolerant of other animals, it's important to use caution and respect each animal's personal boundaries.

To ensure that introductions go smoothly and no one gets hurt, it's generally recommended to introduce the animals on neutral territory. However, you must remember that if your puppy is under 16 weeks of age, you need to be careful about exposing him to dangerous pathogens in the environment. If you can introduce your current pets to your Vizsla outdoors, consider

doing so in an area that is not frequently visited by your current pets. This may be your front yard or a neighbor's yard if you obtain permission. If you must introduce them indoors, try to do so in a room that your current pets don't spend a lot of time in, but be sure that it's big enough to allow all animals their own personal space. Consider using a home office, formal dining room, or guest room.

It's crucial that you restrain each animal during introductions. For dogs, this will mean a collar or harness and leash. A harness will be the best choice for a puppy since he likely won't be leash trained yet, and a harness will be easier and less damaging if you need to grab him quickly and remove him from a situation. If your current dogs are reactive when on a leash, you'll need to proceed with caution, but it's still best if you can safely restrain each animal if possible. If you're introducing your Vizsla to a cat, you should consider restraining the puppy and allowing the cat to move around freely. Cats don't typically tolerate restraint the same way that dogs do. For other types of pets, including pocket pets, birds, or livestock, keeping the puppy on a leash while the other animal remains behind a fence or cage barrier is the ideal option.

If possible, it's best to allow your current pets and your puppy to view each other from afar. If they seem comfortable and there are no signs of fear or aggression, you can allow them to move closer. Throughout the interaction, you need to continue to monitor their body language and be ready to respond should either animal begin to behave fearfully or aggressively.

*Photo Courtesy
of Lee and Jessica Barwick*

Separating the animals or at least giving them more space typically resolves this behavior. For particularly nervous animals, several of these introductory sessions may be required before the two animals can feel comfortable around one another.

Remember, accidents can happen in the blink of an eye, so it's important that you closely monitor any interactions between your Vizsla puppy and your current pets. It can take several months of supervision before you can fully trust them to behave appropriately, but it's important to be cautious to prevent any tragedies from occurring.

Introducing an Adult Dog to Other Animals

If you've brought home an adult Vizsla, you'll need to use more caution when introducing him to your other pets than you would if he were a puppy. Adult dogs tend to be more tolerant of puppies than of other adults, so your current dogs may be less forgiving. Additionally, if you aren't entirely sure of your new Vizsla's past, he may have issues with other pets, especially those of other species. Again, you'll need to closely monitor all animals' body language to ensure that neither one is becoming anxious about the interaction. As with puppies, introducing the animals on neutral territory with proper restraint is recommended.

Again, it's recommended to allow animals to view and smell each other from afar before allowing them closer. Be ready to interrupt any bad behavior, but try to be as calm as possible so that your nervous energy doesn't inspire them to act out. If you're not sure about how to go about introducing your Vizsla to your other pets, or things aren't going according to plan, consider consulting a professional trainer or behaviorist for advice. It's better to seek professional help than risk your pets' safety.

Vizslas and Small Pets

If you have small pets at home, such as cats, rodents, or rabbits, you should always mention it to the breeder or rescue staff prior to committing to adoption. This is especially true if you're bringing home an adult Vizsla. However, if you're bringing home a puppy, prey drive can be a determining factor in which puppy you take home. Once you get home, you'll need to teach your Vizsla how to properly interact with your small pets, if he's allowed to do so at all.

For many dogs, their instinct to pursue prey is triggered by fast movement. Your Vizsla will likely use his strong scenting abilities to gather

Photo Courtesy
of Ashley Tucker

information on the new animal, but he may not actually try to chase until the animal runs from him. This is why restraint during introductions is so important. If your Vizsla gives chase without a collar or harness on, you have little chance of catching him. As noted earlier, Vizslas were not bred to dispatch prey, but this does not mean that your Vizsla won't harm the animal if he's able to catch it.

Allow your Vizsla to interact with small pets only under strict supervision and with restraint. You may also consider not allowing your Vizsla to interact with any small animals at all. It can be relatively easy to keep small pets separated by keeping them in a room with the door closed or with a barrier such as a baby gate. Outdoor pets, such as poultry, may be kept away from the dog with a fence or by having your Vizsla on a leash. If your Vizsla tends to chase your cat, you may need to keep him separated from the cat when you're unable to supervise, in addition to giving the cat a separate area of the house to retreat to.

Managing a home with a Vizsla and small pets is not impossible, but it can be difficult, especially if the dog has a high prey drive. If you're worried about your Vizsla's behavior around your small animals, consult a trainer or behaviorist right away.

Fighting and Bad Behavior

Vizslas are not an aggressive breed, but this does not mean that your new Vizsla won't fight if provoked. Aggression, even on a small scale, should be taken seriously. If the behavior is allowed to escalate to an actual fight, serious injuries and even death can occur. The signs your dog displays in his body language prior to a fight can be subtle, but it's important to notice them so that you can intervene. Dog fights are incredibly dangerous, especially if there is a significant size difference between dogs. It's also common for humans to be injured when breaking up fights, so if you can prevent the fight in the first place, so much the better.

The most common causes of fights between dogs are bullying and resource guarding. If you notice these behaviors between two dogs, you need to intervene immediately and correct the behavior. Dogs should always be allowed to have some personal boundaries, but they should not be allowed to push each other around, play too roughly, or claim toys, furniture, or people as their own. During the initial stages of bad behavior, an interruption such as a clap or stomp or "No!" should be enough to distract the dogs and allow you to redirect their attention.

Watch out for aggressive body language, such as one dog trying to stand over the other. With dogs, height is power, so you may notice one dog holding his head high above the other or attempting to do so from on top of furniture. A tense body, leaning forward slightly with eyes locked on the other animal, is a sign of impending aggression. You may also see raised hackles or bared teeth, but it's important to note that these signs may be incredibly subtle. Some dogs may stiffen slightly while making direct eye contact for just a moment before they attack. It can take some skill to notice these signs, but you need to look for them and intervene immediately when you see them.

It's also helpful if you can take note of what may be triggering the aggressive behavior. If the dogs are playing too roughly, pushing each other around, or guarding items such as food, toys, furniture, or family members, you may be able

FUN FACT
Speed

Vizslas are ranked as one of the fastest dog breeds, with a top-end speed of 64 km or about 39.7 miles per hour. Greyhounds are slightly faster, with a speed of 43–45 miles per hour. For a human reference, the fastest human on earth, Usain Bolt, ran at a top speed of about 27 miles per hour at the height of his career.

to solve the problem more easily than if you aren't sure what could be at the root of the behavior.

If the dogs do end up in a fight, you need to be incredibly cautious about how to break it up. Even the friendliest dogs have been known to redirect onto their owner when they are pulled away from a fight, so never try to separate dogs by grabbing their collars or bodies. If the dogs are not too invested in the fight, it may be easy to break up, but if they are serious, it can take some effort to pull them apart.

At first, you may try hands-off methods of breaking up the fight. This is the only time that you may yell, stomp, clap, or bang metal food dishes together to startle your dogs. Tossing a bowl of water at the dogs or spraying them with a hose may also be enough to distract them from each other. Some owners have also found success in throwing a blanket over the dogs to disorient them.

If these methods do not work, you will need to physically pull the dogs apart. This method is most effective with two people but can be done alone if necessary. Decide which dog is the aggressor and which is simply defending himself. If you have a partner, he or she can take one dog while you take the other. If you are alone, you'll need to grab the aggressor by the back legs and quickly pull him backward or swing him to the side. This action needs to be done quickly to startle the dog and prevent him from redirecting onto you. Once they have been pulled apart, you need to restrain the dogs as quickly as possible so that they cannot return to the fight.

When breaking up a fight, it's possible that you may encounter two dogs that will bite onto each other and refuse to release. Never try to pry a dog's jaws apart with your bare hands, as you will be bitten. If you can find a wedge-shaped object nearby, insert it into the dog's mouth and use it to pry its teeth off the other dog. If this is a concern that you have about your dogs, you can purchase a product called a break stick, which is designed specifically for this purpose. This is a risky maneuver, but may be crucial in saving a dog's life, so make sure that you minimize the risk as much as possible by keeping your hands as far away from the dog's jaws as possible as the dog may try to regrip once he's released his bite.

Aggression to the point of fighting is a serious and challenging problem for the average owner to tackle. If your dog's behavior has progressed to this point, you need to consider seeking professional help as soon as possible. A professional trainer or behaviorist will have far more experience in dealing with aggression and will be able to address the problem and hopefully prevent any injuries or tragedies from occurring.

Raising Multiple Puppies from the Same Litter

If your new Vizsla will be the only pet in your home, it can be tempting to bring home more than one puppy from the same litter. This idea may be appealing as your Vizsla will have a companion that he's known since birth, and you'll save yourself the hassle of introducing a new dog later. However, raising littermates is rarely recommended. Even many professionals are unwilling to attempt such an endeavor.

Raising multiple puppies does not save you any time or effort as you have twice the mess to clean up and twice the time commitment for training, exercise, and socialization. Additionally, you risk having your puppies develop littermate syndrome, a group of behaviors developed by dogs of approximately the same age. Dogs do not have to be littermates, just young and about the same age. Littermate syndrome often manifests in one puppy becoming shy or withdrawn while the other may be more of a bully. Despite any friction between them, the puppies may be incredibly co-dependent and will bond more closely with each other than with any human in the household. Eventually, most cases of littermate syndrome progress to aggressive behavior and fighting between the puppies.

Due to the prevalence of littermate syndrome, it is very rare for a reputable breeder to allow someone to take more than one of their puppies at a time. If you desire a playmate or companion for your Vizsla, it's best to work on one puppy at a time. Focus on training and socializing your dog while also minimizing any separation anxiety. Once you believe that your Vizsla is relatively well trained, you can consider welcoming another dog into your home. Spending one-on-one time with a puppy will encourage him to bond with you rather than another dog, which will allow you to better repeat the process with the second puppy once you're ready.

Options if Your Pets Don't Get Along

Vizslas are typically quite friendly with other pets and tend to get along well in multi-pet homes, but it's always possible that your pets may not get along, no matter how hard you try. Whether it's your current pets causing the problem, or your new Vizsla, it's important to consider your options if they just don't seem to get along. Many older pets can be resistant to change, especially if they've been the sole focus of your attention for a long time, so you will need to allow them extra time to adapt to life with a new dog. Be patient and committed to your training, but if you're struggling, you may need professional help.

Photo Courtesy
of Mark McCrary

If you have tried your hardest and your pets still aren't getting along, you need to make a potentially heartbreaking decision. If you would like to keep two pets that can't be allowed to interact, you'll need to manage them in a way that allows them the same amount of attention, training, and exercise while keeping them entirely separate. This is often referred to as "crate and rotate." Each pet must be allowed to have its own space to retreat to, and you must be willing to commit extra time to ensuring each animal receives its fair share of love and care. This lifestyle can be incredibly time-consuming and emotionally exhausting. Not all owners are able to give their dogs the quality of life they need while keeping them separated, so you will need to consider whether you are willing or able to provide this level of care for the next decade or so of your pets' lives.

If you decide that you can't manage separate lifestyles for each of your pets, you may want to consider rehoming one of them. There is no shame in rehoming an animal if it's in its best interest. It's better to give an animal the life he deserves than to force him to tolerate a life that he's unhappy with. Some pets may prefer to be only animals, while others just need a different type of lifestyle or home environment. The decision to rehome an animal is heartbreaking, but it's crucial to prioritize your pets' well-being over your own feelings. Your pets' happiness is your responsibility, so if you choose to rehome, it's important that you choose wisely or seek the help of a rescue organization or breeder. Remember, the kindest thing you can do for an animal is to make sure that it's cared for and happy, even if this means it must go to another home.

CHAPTER 12
Training your Vizsla

> *Vizslas love to please. They thrive on it. Always praise them when they mind and ignore their behavior when they don't. Be gentle at first with misunderstandings or errors. Try again, use praise, and be sure not to frighten your Vizsla—use patience and repeat, rewarding with love.*
>
> STEPHEN J SHLYEN
> *Rheingold Vizslas*

The Importance of Early Training

No matter how old your new Vizsla is at the time of his arrival in your home, it's important to begin training as soon as possible. Though you should keep your expectations low and allow your new companion time to decompress, beginning training right away helps to establish expectations and build a bond between you. Early training will set your Vizsla up for success and prepare him for life in his new home. By establishing boundaries and expectations early, you will hopefully prevent the development of bad behaviors while also providing the dog with an outlet for mental stimulation.

During the early stages of training, it's important to keep it positive. This may mean that your training sessions last as little as three to five minutes. Puppies typically do not have a long attention span, so it's important to keep your training sessions short and quit before your dog loses focus. This is true for adult dogs as well, but they can generally train for a bit longer than puppies. Quitting before the dog loses interest will keep him engaged and looking forward to the next session. To encourage him further, it's also important that you always end on a good note. If he's becoming frustrated or confused at what you're asking him to do, go back to something he knows and have him perform that behavior a few times so that you can reward him.

End the session there and return to the difficult task at a later time. Your Vizsla may just need time to think about it and to rest his mind and body.

By keeping training sessions short and interesting, you're also establishing a positive outlook on training with your new dog. These early training sessions will set the tone for your working relationship with your dog, so it's important to do your best to make sure that he's having a good time. Training can be frustrating at times, but try not to get too discouraged during the first few weeks or months with your dog. As always, if you need help with training at any stage, don't be afraid to seek professional help.

> "
>
> *A Vizsla is extremely smart and learns quickly, so do not assume that, just because it is young, you have to wait before you start any training. I always talk about how you can lift the lid of a dog treat jar and hear it make a sound. The next time you lift that lid, your Vizsla pup will come running to get a treat. They learn that quickly.*
>
> **LINDA AND JIM BUSCH**
> *Busch Vizslas*
> "

Operant Conditioning Basics

If you are not familiar with the term already, operant conditioning is a method of learning originally devised and promoted by American behaviorist and psychologist B.F. Skinner, who based his work on the idea that humans and animals are far too complex to learn through classical conditioning alone. Skinner believed that if certain behaviors were followed with a positive experience, the person or animal would be more likely to repeat the behavior in the future, whereas if the behavior were followed by a negative experience, the learner would be less likely to perform the behavior again.

B.F. Skinner believed that there are three types of environmental responses that are capable of shaping a learner's behavior. The three responses include neutral operants, punishments, and reinforcers. Neutral operants do not influence a learner's behavior and do not increase or decrease the likelihood of the behavior being repeated in the future. For example, if your dog begins barking and your response is to continue scrolling on your phone, your behavior could be considered a neutral operant

Photo Courtesy
of Maddi Sparkes

as it has no effect on your dog's behavior. Punishments, as you may have guessed, will discourage a learner from repeating a behavior, while reinforcers will encourage a certain behavior. Reinforcers may be either positive or negative, but both result in a positive outcome for the learner.

Positive reinforcements include food, verbal praise, play, and affection. These reinforcers are most frequently used in dog training since most dogs are motivated by food, affection, or toys. However, positive reinforcement may also be used inadvertently to encourage bad behaviors. For example, a dog that digs out of the backyard and is rewarded with an exhilarating romp around the neighborhood will be more likely to try again after you fill in the hole. A dog that gets into the trash and manages to find some tasty snacks will probably get into the trash again in the future. These types of behaviors are best prevented as they are self-rewarding and can be particularly difficult habits to break.

Negative reinforcement is often misunderstood in dog training and is not to be confused with punishment. In fact, many owners use negative reinforcement without even realizing what they are doing. Negative reinforcement is simply the removal of an unpleasant sensation. For example, if you place gentle pressure on the leash and release that pressure as soon as your Vizsla moves in the desired direction, you are using negative reinforcement. This is not a cruel training method; it's simply teaching the dog that he can remove the leash pressure by moving in the direction you want. Negative reinforcement is also frequently combined with positive reinforcement for maximum efficacy. The release of that leash pressure combined with a tasty treat will quickly help the dog learn not to brace against the leash and instead follow where you want him to go.

Punishment is a different concept as it is meant to discourage the dog from performing a specific behavior. Punishments can range from slightly unpleasant to cruel, and caution must be taken if you use them, as harsh punishments are often damaging to a dog's mind and body. A mild punishment may include a loud noise, such as a clap, stomp, or "No!" Those noises won't harm the dog but are enough

Photo Courtesy of John Brown

124

to startle him and leave him with an unpleasant experience. Painful punishments should be avoided at all costs as they can cause lasting harmful effects. Vizslas are sensitive dogs that respond badly to harsh punishments, which can leave the dog with lasting physical or mental trauma. No matter how badly your Vizsla behaves, it's never appropriate to hit or kick him.

> *Vizslas want to make their owners happy. If you are trying to train your dog for a particular task and he is not mastering it, try to think of a different way to train him. We have raised Vizslas for 17 years, and what has worked on the last four generations may not work on your newest pup. Patience is always the key. He will feed off your energy, both positive and negative. A hard hand will ruin your Vizsla. You can easily hurt a Vizsla's feelings, and that is a hard thing to mend. Short training sessions that end positively work best.*
>
> **LISA WEST**
> *Red Sky Kennel*

Essential Commands

Vizslas are an intelligent breed, so they're typically quite easy to train. As long as you maintain a gentle approach to training, there is really no limit to what you can teach your dog. However, there are a few essential commands that are useful for every dog to know. Once your Vizsla has mastered the basics, you can move on to more advanced or sport-specific commands. Skills such as walking on a loose leash, recognizing his name, and sitting and lying down are useful in a variety of situations and may even be used on a daily basis. Once your Vizsla has mastered these foundational skills, you can use them to build your dog's skill base and explore the nearly limitless training opportunities that follow.

Name Recognition

One of the first skills you need to teach your Vizsla is to recognize his given name. If you've brought home an adult Vizsla, he may already have a name that he recognizes. If you've adopted a puppy or plan on changing your adult dog's name, you'll need to teach him to respond to his new moniker. Name recognition is an essential skill that will be used in a wide variety of training situations, so it's an ideal place to start once you bring your Vizsla home.

Ideally, you should start in a quiet environment with your Vizsla on a leash so he can't wander off should he become distracted. Wave a delicious treat in front of your dog's face to get him to focus on you. Say his name and immediately reward him with the treat. Repeat this process several times, pairing his name with a treat each time. After a few repetitions, you can let him go back to whatever he was doing—but be sure to repeat these sessions frequently. As your Vizsla progresses, he'll understand that his name means that he should focus on you for a delicious reward. With practice, you can phase out the treats and reward with affection or praise.

Sit

The sit command is one that you may find yourself using as frequently as every day. You may ask your Vizsla to sit politely while you put his collar or harness on, or you may want him to sit while you set his food bowl down. If you plan on competing in dog sports, you'll also need this command for a variety of disciplines. Additionally, the sit can be built upon to teach other commands such as stay, lie down, or sit pretty.

There are two methods of teaching your Vizsla to sit on command. The first uses positive reinforcement only, while the second uses both positive and negative reinforcement. Depending on your dog, you may find one method works better than the other. There is no definitive method of training dogs, so do what works best for you and your Vizsla.

It's helpful to keep your Vizsla on a leash to prevent him from wandering away mid-session, but if you are in a particularly quiet environment, you may not need a leash. Gain your Vizsla's attention with a high-value treat or by saying his name. Lure him into position by moving the treat from in front of his face to above his head. You want the treat high enough he can't quite reach it, but not so high that he tries to jump up. At first, he may try to back up or jump up, but be patient as he figures out what you're asking. It's not recommended to attach a verbal cue until the dog begins to understand the task. The moment his hind end touches the ground, reward him with the treat and plenty of praise.

*Photo Courtesy
of Logan Hammingh*

If your Vizsla is struggling with the sit, you may consider adding negative reinforcement. This can be done in two ways. First, you can apply gentle pressure on your dog's rear end while you lure him into position. Don't push his hind end down, but maintain constant gentle pressure to encourage him to move away from it. If he moves to the side, simply try again. When combined with the treat overhead, he should quickly understand that sitting will relieve the pressure and gain him a reward. Alternatively, you can perform this same process but with gentle upward pressure on the leash. Do not pull the leash or maintain enough pressure to affect your dog's breathing, as the pressure should be mild but constant. With both methods, you must release the pressure the moment your Vizsla begins to sit.

Lie Down

As with sit, the lie down command can be used in numerous everyday situations. It can also be used as the foundation for stay, as well as fun tricks like roll over or play dead. If you plan on competing with your Vizsla, the lie down command is also required in many dog sports.

While your Vizsla doesn't necessarily need to know how to sit before you teach lie down, it can be helpful. Again, you may want to have him on a leash to prevent him from wandering off mid-session. Ask your Vizsla to sit, if he can, and gain his attention with a high-value treat. Lure him down to the ground by bringing the treat down and slightly in front of him. Your Vizsla may lie down right away, or he may stand and put his head down. If he stands, simply return him to the original position and try again. The moment his elbows touch the ground, reward him with the treat and a lot of praise. Once he begins to understand what you want, you can also introduce a verbal command.

Negative reinforcement can also be used to teach your Vizsla to lie down. Use gentle downward pressure on the leash to encourage your dog to lie down as you lure him into position with the treat. Your Vizsla may react by moving away or bracing against the pressure. But maintain that same gentle pressure until he lies down. The pressure needs to be gentle but flexible, as you don't want to create a solid barrier with the collar and leash that could cause your dog to panic. Never stand on the leash with pressure as this creates a solid barrier with more intense pressure, and a sensitive Vizsla will not respond well. However, a little gentle downward pressure combined with the tasty treat should be enough to convince your Vizsla to lie down. Again, once he begins moving downward, immediately release the pressure and reward him once he's all the way down.

Photo Courtesy
of Megan Halfhill

Stay

In addition to being a requirement in many dog sports, the stay command can be incredibly useful in teaching your Vizsla both patience and respect. There are two versions of the stay that you may want to differentiate between in your training. Some trainers use the word "stay" for a longer duration where the handler returns to the dog's side to release him, as can be seen in competitive obedience. The command "wait" is used for shorter periods of time where the dog can be released at a distance if needed, such as during recall training or after setting a food bowl on the ground.

Though you should teach your Vizsla to stay in a variety of positions, you should begin with whatever your dog is most comfortable with. Most dogs begin in either a sit or down, but standing is acceptable as well. However, standing sometimes encourages novice dogs to walk away, so you may want to encourage your dog to sit or lie down, even if he prefers to stand. Once he is in position, wait a few seconds before rewarding him. Again, you don't need to introduce the verbal command until he has a better understanding of what you're asking him to do.

As your Vizsla better understands your expectations of him, you can ask for longer durations, and you can introduce movement. Start by taking one step to the side or away from your dog. Return to his side and reward him for staying in position. Increase that distance as your dog advances, and consider introducing distractions such as people or other dogs, treats or toys being tossed, or leaving the room entirely. If at any point your Vizsla moves out of his stay, simply return him to his original position and try again. If he is consistently moving, you will need to decrease the duration or return to a less distracting environment.

Recall

The recall is one of the most important commands to teach your Vizsla. Not only will it be useful around the house, but you can use it any time you have your Vizsla off-leash. A solid recall could even save your Vizsla's life someday. Until your Vizsla has mastered this command and has reasonable

FUN FACT
AKC Triple Champ

In 1980 a Vizsla became the first dog to become an AKC Triple Champion by winning the Champion of Record title in field, show, and obedience. The champion Vizsla's name was Kai, and his owners were Robert and Marianne Costa.

Photo Courtesy
of Clayton Schrey

impulse control around small prey animals, it's not recommended to allow him off-leash in unfenced areas.

Teaching the recall is best done with another person, so ask a friend or family member to help you if possible. You should start this training in a quiet environment with few distractions. This training can be done off-leash if the area is fenced, or you can have your dog wear a long line.

Ask your helper to hold your Vizsla as you walk a short distance away. Even a distance of five to ten feet will be enough during the initial stages of training. Call your dog's name to gain his attention if he's not already looking at you. Ask him to come to you using your most excited voice and gestures. You can even have his favorite toy or treat with you. Your helper should hold your dog for a moment to help build his excitement before releasing. Once your dog is on his way to you, run backward a few steps, if possible, to further encourage him to chase you. After he's reached you, you can reward him with the toy or treat and plenty of praise. The process can then be repeated with your helper calling the dog to them or with you returning him to your helper for another attempt. Remember, short sessions are best so that you don't tire your Vizsla out. As he gains understanding of this concept, you can increase the distance and distractions around you.

Drop It

It's never recommended to try to take an object from a dog's mouth, as you risk getting bitten. Even if your Vizsla does not typically display resource-guarding behavior, he can get overexcited trying to get the object back and may accidentally bite your hand. However, it's important to be able to take items from your dog's mouth, both at home and away, so you need to teach him to give up the item when asked.

To teach your Vizsla to give up an item, you need an item of higher value. This may be a treat, toy, or edible chew. Show him the item to draw his attention and lure him away from the item he already has. Once he drops the item, quickly grab it from him. If it's something he's allowed to have, you can give it back to him and repeat the process. With practice, you can begin introducing the verbal command.

Leave It

The leave it command is a useful skill for your Vizsla to have as it may keep him out of trouble. If your dog gets distracted by the neighbor's Poodle or sees a tasty but disgusting snack on the ground, you can tell him to leave it and walk away. Teaching this command requires a high-value treat, so be sure to have your Vizsla's favorite snack on hand.

When your Vizsla sees something that interests him, show him a treat while simultaneously luring him away from the object of interest. If it's a high enough value treat, he should gladly follow you for the food. Once he refocuses on you rather than the object, reward him. If he returns his focus to the distraction, do it again. With practice, you should be able to have him focus on you and walk several steps away or more before rewarding. As he begins to understand what you're asking, you can introduce a verbal command. Once he is reliable, you can begin to phase out the treat and use only the verbal command, and offer praise and affection for a reward.

Take every opportunity daily as a teaching lesson, such as 'sit' before giving meals, 'stay' when opening an exterior door, recalling to a front sit when you don't see where he is, and 'find' your named toy.

LINDA MAUS
MausHaus Vizslas

Advanced Commands

Depending on the goals you have for your Vizsla, your next step in training could be sport-specific. If you're not sure what to work on next, consider signing up for a class. An obedience class or agility foundation class may be just what you need to keep you and your dog busy and interested in working together. More information on different dog sports is provided in Chapter 14.

You may also want to teach your Vizsla fun tricks to entertain you and your family. The AKC has created a Trick Dog program where dogs can earn titles for performing a wide range of tricks. In total, there are five titles that may be earned, with an increasing level of difficulty for each one. If tricks and sports do not appeal to you, you can always work on the difficulty of the basic commands listed here. Increase the duration of your stays or the distance of your recalls. You can also work on basic commands in increasingly distracting environments.

As previously mentioned, Vizslas are intelligent dogs, but they tend to respond best to short and interesting training sessions. The more frequently you can leave your dog wanting more, the more engaged he'll be in the next session. If you or your dog are getting frustrated with a task, return to a simpler command and practice that for a few repetitions and return to the more difficult task in a later session. That will give you time to reflect on what went wrong while also giving your Vizsla a much-needed mental break. The most important aspect of training your Vizsla is to have fun, so make sure you're both enjoying your time together.

CHAPTER 13
Nutrition

> *Feed a quality brand puppy food three times daily for the first year. You can supplement this diet with a little cooked meat and veggies if you like. I find that quality dry kibble contains all the nutrients needed for proper growth, and any added meat/veggies are a nice extra. A puppy should be more on the plump side rather than too thin. One should not be seeing ribs, hips, or back bones; spines should be level. Legs should be straight; stools should not be loose. Base the amount of food given on the activity level and individual need of your puppy. Don't switch brands or type of food. Whereas humans like variety in our meals, dogs do not. Their digestion prefers the same food meal after meal. When in doubt, ask your breeder or veterinarian for suggestions.*
>
> **LINDA MAUS**
> *MausHaus Vizslas*

The Importance of a Balanced Diet

Though the need for a nutritious diet may seem obvious, it's important to understand what makes a diet balanced and how that can affect your Vizsla's health. A nutrient imbalance can cause serious health problems for a Vizsla of any age, but growing puppies are especially at risk for incorrect development. The effects of nutritional imbalances are not generally visible right away, so a dog being fed incorrectly may remain healthy for several weeks or months before any signs of malnourishment becomes apparent. While some of the effects of malnutrition can be repaired, some can be permanent, so it's crucial that your Vizsla eats a balanced diet throughout his life.

The second most important aspect of a proper diet is portion size. Obesity is the most common health issue facing adult dogs of all breeds. Excess weight puts unnecessary strain on your Vizsla's joints, which can be particularly harmful to young puppies and aging seniors. The result of this extra wear and tear on your dog's joints can be as serious as limited mobility and a shorter lifespan. Weight management will be discussed in more detail later in the chapter, but it's important to monitor your Vizsla's weight regularly and adjust his food portions as needed.

Photo Courtesy of Diana Vargas

Basic Nutrition

Canine nutrition is an incredibly complex subject that many profession-als spend their entire careers researching. Though this book will not cover the more complex aspects of nutrition, the basics of canine nutrition will be discussed. Your veterinarian is a great resource to turn to if you have any simple questions about your Vizsla's weight or diet, but most veterinarians have limited knowledge on the subject. It's recommended you consult with a veterinary nutritionist if you have any serious concerns regarding your Vizsla's diet. The American College of Veterinary Nutrition (ACVN) maintains a directory of board-certified veterinary nutritionists in the US and abroad. The list is searchable by location and specialty, so you can find the contact information for the right nutritionist for your situation and location.

Proteins and Amino Acids

Amino acids and protein share a complex role in terms of your Vizsla's diet. During the process of digestion, the proteins contained in your dog's food are broken down into amino acids. The body then uses those amino acids to recombine into different protein molecules that are then used for cell growth, maintenance, and repair. Protein is an essential part of any dog's diet, as it's estimated that approximately 30 percent of a dog's daily protein intake is used just for maintenance of the cells in his coat. Protein is also critical in building and maintaining healthy cells in your Vizsla's skin, tendons, muscles, cartilage, and ligaments. Additionally, protein helps the body main-tain a healthy level of hormone production.

A dog needs 20 amino acids for proper cell growth, maintenance, and repair. About half can be produced by the body, but the rest need to be sup-plied by the diet. These latter amino acids are called essential amino acids.

The ten essential amino acids are:

- Arginine
- Histidine
- Isoleucine
- Leucine
- Lysine
- Methionine
- Phenylalanine
- Threonine
- Tryptophan
- Valine

The protein and amino acids required by your Vizsla are most commonly found in foods containing animal proteins, such as muscle meat, eggs, and dairy products. Plants contain some protein, but not enough for a dog to be able to truly thrive. For this reason, a balanced diet should contain mostly animal-based ingredients with just a few plant-based ingredients. Dogs are not obligate carnivores, so they are able to digest some plant material, but vegetarian and vegan diets are not biologically appropriate and should not be fed.

Photo Courtesy of Mark McCrary

Fat and Fatty Acids

Fat is an important ingredient in any dog's diet. Vitamins A, D, E, and K are fat-soluble vitamins, which means they can only be broken down by fat prior to absorption by the body. Most dogs find fatty diets to be more palatable than low-fat diets, but an excess of fat in the diet can lead to weight gain and pancreatitis. For this reason, a diet must contain an appropriate balance of protein, fat, and carbohydrates. Though protein is an important aspect of your Vizsla's diet, fat is the most concentrated energy source for dogs and is the main source of calories and essential fatty acids. Calories are nothing more than a unit used to measure energy, but an excess of calories can cause weight gain. Like essential amino acids, essential fatty acids are required for healthy cell growth and maintenance but must be supplied by the diet.

The essential fatty acids are:

● Arachidonic acid
● Linoleic acid
● Linolenic acid

The importance of omega-3 and omega-6 fatty acids should also be mentioned. These fatty acids are crucial to your Vizsla's overall health but must be consumed in an appropriate ratio. The ideal ratio is 4:1 with more omega-6s than omega-3s. Linolenic acid provides the body with omega-3 fatty acids, while omega-6s are provided by linoleic acid. Omega-9 fatty acids cannot be used by dogs and may decrease the concentration of omega-3s and -6s, so their consumption should be limited.

Carbohydrates

When it comes to canine nutrition, carbohydrates are a somewhat controversial topic. Carbs are a source of energy but are not the most digestible or nutrient-dense option. Some people choose to exclude carbohydrate-heavy vegetables and grains from their dogs' diets, while commercially produced diets, especially kibble, rely on carbs as a filler to bring down the overall cost of the product. For owners that opt to make their dogs' food at home, carbohydrates are optional, so long as the diet remains nutritionally balanced.

In order for carbohydrates to be used by your Vizsla's body, they must be broken down by the digestive system into glucose. However, it's important to note that many carbs, such as starchy vegetables, can be difficult for dogs to digest unless they are cooked or pureed first. Many vegetables also provide the dog with important antioxidants, phytochemicals, and minerals. Vegetables can also be a great source of dietary fiber.

Feeding Puppies vs. Adult Dogs

Let your puppy eat. They are a high energy breed, and you will be working at putting weight on your dog, more so than having it lose weight. Don't worry about the amount the package says; the dog will eat more than it recommends.

LISA WEST
Red Sky Kennel

> "
>
> *Once a Vizsla has passed its early fast growth, it often starts to skip meals or to not eat all its food. DON'T WORRY; they are very good at regulating what they need for intake. Cut back on amounts until you find a consistent amount that he is willing to eat. Don't doctor up or change foods; your dog will eat what he needs—if only we humans had that willpower.*
>
> **WENDY RUSSELL**
> *Widdershins*
>
> "

Your Vizsla's nutritional needs will inevitably change as he grows and ages, so you will need to adjust his diet accordingly. The idea of a dog eating the same food for its entire life may sound convenient, but it's not ideal. As you search for the perfect food for your Vizsla, you may notice that some dog foods are labeled for dogs in "all life stages." This label means that it has met the nutritional standards set by the Association of American Feed Control Officials for dogs of any age. Food that is appropriate for all life stages will provide the nutrients needed for your Vizsla to remain healthy but will not provide for optimum growth or health. Other foods will be labeled for use with puppies or senior dogs. Puppy foods often have a higher caloric content and contain nutrients needed during critical stages of development. Senior dog foods typically contain fewer calories to accommodate slowing metabolisms, as well as ingredients to support digestive and joint health.

Choosing the correct diet for your Vizsla will involve an evaluation of his age and lifestyle. Most Vizslas will do well on a diet formulated for puppies until they reach about 12 months of age. At that point, they can be switched to an adult maintenance or all life stages food. Particularly active adult Vizslas will likely need a high-performance diet or a much larger portion of food than sedentary Vizslas. As your dog ages and his metabolism and activity level begins to slow down, you may consider switching him to a senior food.

It's important to note that Vizslas that have been spayed or neutered typically require fewer calories per day than unaltered Vizslas. Additionally, pregnant or lactating Vizslas require more calories than the average adult dog and may need to be fed a more nutrient-dense food until their puppies have been weaned. It's also worth noting that if you have multiple dogs in your home, there may be times where you will need to buy different types of food for each dog. This can seem like a hassle, but it's the best way to ensure that each dog is receiving the correct diet he needs to thrive.

Commercial Diets

> *I feed nothing but Purina Pro Plan Sport dog food to my Vizslas from the time they're weaned off of their mother's milk, throughout their lives. It is a 30% protein/20% fat formula and highly digestible. It is the best dog food I've found, and my dogs do great on it and maintain an ideal body weight.*
>
> **DENZIL RAY COOPER**
> *Cooper's Redneck Kennel*

Kibble is the most common type of commercial diet fed by dog owners of any breed. Kibble is popular because it's readily available in nearly all areas of the country, and it's budget-friendly and easy to store and feed. It's available in a wide range of formulas, making it ideal for dogs of all ages, including those with food sensitivities and health problems. Some kibble is made with grains, while others are made without. Different proteins are also available, such as chicken, beef, and lamb. Novel proteins such as kangaroo, venison, and salmon can also be found to suit dogs with allergies or sensitivities. Kibble formulated for dogs with specific health issues may be available by prescription only. However, no matter what your budget is, there is a kibble to suit your dog's unique needs and lifestyle.

There has been some controversy recently regarding grain-free kibble. Ingredients such as corn, wheat, and soy are often blamed as the source of many dogs' allergies and sensitivities. In response, many dog food manufacturers have begun producing food with different carbohydrates such as peas or potatoes. In recent years, a potential link between these new grain-free foods and a heart disease called dilated cardiomyopathy, or DCM, has emerged. The connection between grain-free foods and DCM has not yet been proven, but some veterinarians have begun discouraging owners from feeding grain-free kibble. Again, the research is ongoing, and no direct connection has been found. But if you are unsure whether grain-free kibble is appropriate for your Vizsla, it's best to discuss the matter with your veterinarian.

Another commercial diet option is canned food. Canned food is just as readily available and easy to store and feed as kibble, but it's softer and more palatable than kibble. It's often a great addition for dogs who are picky eaters or those who need to gain some weight. It's also higher in moisture, so it's often suggested for dogs that don't drink enough water on their own. Canned food is also available in a wide variety of formulas to suit the needs of most dogs. However, canned food is more calorie-dense than many brands of kibble, so correct portion size is essential. It also tends to stick to teeth more than dry food, so your Vizsla may need more frequent dental cleanings if he eats much canned food.

One of the newest commercially available diets is fresh-cooked dog food. This type of food is frequently found in the refrigerated section of your local pet or grocery store. Some online companies also cater to their customers by sending their food straight to their doorstep. Fresh-cooked food is usually packaged in a roll and is fed by slicing off the correct portion size. The roll can then be rewrapped and returned to the fridge until the next use. Fresh-cooked dog food is often ideal for Vizsla owners who want to give their dogs a fresher meal than kibble or canned food but without the expense or effort of a homemade diet.

Many Vizsla owners are now turning to more natural diet options for their dogs, but without the effort of a homemade diet. Commercially available raw diets have filled this niche, though it is usually the most expensive type of commercial diet. Raw foods are made from a nutritionally balanced combination of muscle meat, bone, and organ, with smaller amounts of fruits and vegetables. Most raw diets contain little to no grains and are stored in the freezer until ready to use. Raw food is available in a range of proteins, but it is also available in different portion sizes, including small, easy-to-thaw pellets, medium-sized nuggets, and large patties.

Homemade Diets

> 66
>
> *For a Vizsla, good nutrition consists of fat and protein. Consider mixing in a small amount of bacon fat with meals. We use a high fat/protein kibble, mixed with pressure-cooked chicken leg quarters with carrots, celery, and some garlic flavoring. Be creative with the vegetables mixed in.*
>
> **STEPHEN J SHLYEN**
> *Rheingold Vizslas*
>
> 99

If you have the time and budget available, you may want to consider making your Vizsla's food at home. However, it's important to note that commercial dog food is required by law to meet specific nutritional standards, so you always know you're feeding a balanced diet. With homemade dog food, it's your responsibility to make sure that you're providing your dog with the necessary nutrients.

If you are considering feeding your Vizsla a homemade diet, it would be wise to seek the advice of a professional canine nutritionist. You may be able to find a nutritionist near you, or you may choose to find one that provides virtual assistance via phone calls, Zoom, or emails. The ACVN publishes a list of veterinary nutritionists on its website. Though the organization is American, the list includes nutritionists all over the world, so you should be able to find one to provide local or remote guidance. A professional canine nutritionist will evaluate your Vizsla's overall health, as well as his age and lifestyle, to formulate a balanced recipe you can make at home.

The most popular type of homemade diet is raw, which is frequently divided into two categories: BARF, or biologically appropriate raw food, and PMR, or prey model raw. PMR diets are also sometimes called ratio diets, as they are designed to follow the approximate ratio of muscle meat, bone, and organ provided by the average prey animal. PMR diets are meant to simulate the diet of the wild ancestors of modern dogs. The most common ratio used is 80% muscle meat, 10% bone, 10% liver, and 10% other secreting organs. Fruits and vegetables are optional, and some owners choose to skip them entirely.

BARF diets are similar but tend to use more vegetable matter and even some grains and starchy vegetables, such as potato, barley, oats, or rice. Additives such as bone broth, fermented fish stock, and raw goat's milk are also used with both PMR and BARF diets. Though the guidelines for these diets may seem simple, it's important to note that both ratio and BARF diets lack specific nutrients such as zinc, vitamin E, and manganese. For this reason, most experienced raw feeders recommend working with a veterinary nutritionist to formulate a balanced raw recipe for your Vizsla's unique needs.

Cooked diets are another popular homemade option frequently used by owners who aren't comfortable feeding a fully raw diet. Some dogs may also prefer cooked over raw. In most cooked diets, the ingredients are similar to those used in raw diets, but they are baked or boiled prior to serving. Most cooked diets are also heavier in carbs than raw diets and may include barley, rice, or oats as a base. The most notable difference between cooked and raw diets is that cooked diets do not incorporate bones. Raw bones do

FUN FACT
A Vizsla Hero

Bart was the first Vizsla ever to be awarded the American Kennel Club Award for Canine Excellence (ACE) in 2013. After developing a limp, Bart was diagnosed with bone cancer that had already eaten away 80 percent of his scapula. One of his front legs was amputated, and he underwent chemotherapy, after which he went on to earn the Master Hunter title. In addition, Bart participated in events with the Wounded Warrior Project and helped inspire veterans who returned from war with missing limbs to live their lives to the fullest. Bart's osteosarcoma was in remission for six years, after which he succumbed to the disease.

not splinter in the same manner as cooked bones, so they are considered safe to feed. Cooked bones are dangerous and should not be fed, so cooked diets typically use powdered calcium supplements such as seaweed calcium or ground eggshells.

If your homemade diet of choice does use raw bones, you'll need to follow safe feeding guidelines. Weight-bearing bones of large animals like cattle are dense enough that they can cause a dog to break or chip teeth. Dogs have also been known to wedge marrow bones over their lower jaws or attempt to swallow smaller bones whole. If your Vizsla is a heavy chewer, it's recommended to only give him softer bones so that he won't damage his teeth. A Vizsla prone to gulping should only be given bones big enough that he can't swallow it whole. Whenever you give your dog a bone to eat or chew on, supervise him the entire time. It takes only a moment for a dog to choke or injure himself, so you need to be there to intervene if necessary. If your Vizsla is prone to gulping his food, consider grinding the bones into his food or use a powdered calcium supplement.

There are other risks with homemade diets to be aware of. The most important risk to be aware of comes with the handling of raw meat. Dogs' digestive systems are very different from ours, and they can typically handle small amounts of pathogens such as salmonella in their food. Humans, however, can get very sick if they consume something contaminated with salmonella, so you need to be careful about handling your Vizsla's raw food.

If you have any immunocompromised family members in the household, you'll need to be especially cautious about your food handling practices. Be sure to clean your prep area thoroughly, even if you're preparing a cooked diet. Even meat intended for human consumption can be contaminated, so you need to clean well. You should also restrict your dog's access to your house when eating. Feeding him in a kennel will result in a much easier cleanup than if you allow him to drag a chicken neck through the house. Furniture and carpet can be incredibly difficult to clean, so limit him to eating on easy to clean surfaces only. If the weather is nice, you can feed him outside or lay down towels in a playpen or kennel.

You can also wipe your Vizsla's face and paws after he's finished eating to help prevent the spread of harmful bacteria. Remember, many owners feed their dogs raw diets without incidence, but it's crucial to prioritize the safety of both your dog and other family members.

Weight Management

> With an adult Vizsla we like to see the shadow of three small ribs on the chest. After dinner, Vizslas seem to disappear until the next meal. Look for thighs and forearms to muscle up. Consider this: When you look over the back of your dog, you will want to see a waist just between the rib cage and the hind end. Too much weight might generate too much pressure on the feet and cause the feet to splay. Vizslas should have catlike feet, not splayed-out toes. Your feeding and exercise will determine your dog's health.
>
> STEPHEN J SHLYEN
> *Rheingold Vizslas*

In 2018, the Association for Pet Obesity Prevention performed a study that revealed that approximately 56% of dogs in the United States were overweight or obese. Of those dogs, 90% of their owners did not recognize that their dogs were above a healthy weight. Some owners may recognize that their dogs are overweight, but they may not realize the detrimental effects that weight can have on their dogs' bodies.

Though the AKC breed standard states that Vizslas should weigh between 44 and 60 pounds, that doesn't mean that your dog is a healthy weight if he is within that range. A small Vizsla who would be healthy at 44 pounds would be considered obese at 60 pounds. The breed standard is helpful in determining whether a dog is the proper size but not the proper weight. If you need help determining whether your Vizsla is the correct weight for his size, it's best to ask your veterinarian at your dog's next checkup.

Photo Courtesy
of Samantha M. D'Anna

One of the most important and often overlooked aspects of weight management is proper portion sizes. It's all too easy to consider the amount of food you give your Vizsla for breakfast and dinner while overlooking all of the training treats, chews, and snacks he may receive in between. If you're feeding a commercial diet, you may be aware of the feeding guidelines on the packaging. These should always be considered rough guidelines that should be adjusted according to each dog's individual needs. If your Vizsla could lose a few pounds, consider cutting back on meal sizes as well as treats during the day. You can also switch your dog's normal food for a low-calorie option and opt for low-calorie training treats or vegetables. You can always feed your Vizsla his entire breakfast during a morning training session and his dinner during an evening training session if you'd like to cut back while still maintaining his training schedule.

Physical exercise is the other key to proper weight management. Simply put, the more active your Vizsla is, the more food he'll be able to eat each day without excess weight gain. If your Vizsla is overweight, you'll need to not only limit his portion sizes but increase his daily exercise as well. Just be sure to start slowly as he may not have much fitness if he has led a sedentary life until that point. A well-exercised dog will be a tired dog that is more likely to stay out of trouble too.

Food Allergies and Intolerances

Though relatively rare, it's not unheard of for Vizslas to develop food allergies or intolerances. Food is one of the most common causes of allergies or hypersensitivities in all breeds of dogs. Food allergies are the result of an overreaction of the dog's immune system due to the presence of certain proteins in the body. Depending on the severity of the reaction, it may be referred to as an allergy or intolerance. Digestive upset and generalized itching are common symptoms, but dogs may also experience ear and skin infections, vomiting, and diarrhea. Dogs' immune systems can react to any ingredient in food, but the most common allergens are beef, chicken, lamb, corn, soy, and wheat.

The diagnosis of allergies and intolerances is not a simple process, so if you suspect your Vizsla may have issues with his food, be prepared for a long journey toward healing. Unfortunately, allergy tests aren't completely reliable, so your vet may recommend an elimination diet. Elimination diets can take many weeks or months to get a reliable answer, so patience is key. On an elimination diet, dogs are fed a food containing a novel protein such as kangaroo, venison, or salmon. These proteins are uncommon in dog foods, so they are less likely to result in an allergic reaction. Limited ingredients in the diet will also be essential. After the dog eats this food for a few weeks, you can determine whether he is reacting to the ingredients or if he's tolerating it well. If he seems fine, you can introduce a new protein and feed that for a few weeks. A few weeks on each protein is necessary to give the immune system enough time to react if it's going to do so.

It's also possible that your Vizsla may have a reaction to any number of different proteins, which can make it more difficult to obtain an answer. If you can't seem to find a food that your dog won't react to, you may need to opt for a hypoallergenic diet, which is typically only available by prescription. These types of dog food contain hydrolyzed proteins, which are broken down into such small particles as to bypass the immune system. However, hypoallergenic diets are generally considered a last resort for many owners as they are often prohibitively expensive.

Performance and Sport Dog Nutrition

If your Vizsla is a particularly active dog that regularly participates in strenuous physical activities, you'll need to adjust his diet to ensure that he's receiving the right nutrition. Activities such as hunting, joring, running,

and agility are physically and metabolically demanding on any dog's body. The main concern with feeding performance and sport dogs is ensuring that the dog is receiving enough calories per day. Many performance dog handlers recommend a high protein diet, though not all dogs can tolerate high levels of protein. A food containing between 25% and 40% protein is typically recommended for highly active dogs. Higher fat levels are also recommended, though caution should be taken as high fat may also cause pancreatitis in some dogs.

Highly active Vizslas should also be provided with a constant source of clean and fresh water, especially if they are being fed a high protein diet. High protein diets require more water for the removal of excess nitrogen, so it's important that the dog is able to drink enough. If you're worried about your Vizsla not consuming enough water each day, you may consider feeding him a diet containing more moisture, such as raw or canned food.

Depending on the type of activity your Vizsla is performing, you may want to consider working with a canine nutritionist specializing in work with canine athletes. That way, you can be sure that your dog is receiving the right balance of nutrients to allow him to perform at the top of his game.

CHAPTER 14
Physical and Mental Exercise

"

There's a fine line between 'wearing them out' and 'building endurance.' You always want to exercise your dog just enough to take the edge off, and wear him out the rest of the way using his brain!

MICHEL BERNER
Mira Vizslas

"

The Importance of Physical Exercise

Physical exercise should be an important part of every Vizsla's daily schedule. Exercise will not only assist in keeping your dog at a healthy weight, but it will help prevent him from developing boredom-related bad behaviors. A Vizsla with too much pent-up energy will find his own ways to entertain and exercise himself, but it's typically not in a way that's approved by his owners.

The ideal amount of daily physical activity needed by your Vizsla will depend on his age, health, and overall energy level. Some Vizslas will be satisfied with a long walk and perhaps a short training session or game of fetch, while others may need significantly more exercise. Though puppies and seniors may need a fair amount of exercise each day, they will not have the stamina of a healthy adult dog, so you may need to exercise your dog in shorter sessions throughout the day. In general, a healthy adult Vizsla will need at least an hour of physical and mental exercise each day. However, this is just a guideline, and your individual dog may have different needs, especially if he has any health or mobility problems.

It's also important to note that this does not mean you need to run your Vizsla for an hour straight each day. If that's what you and your Vizsla enjoy, that's great, but you can also break it up into shorter sessions throughout the day. For example, if you only have time for a 30-minute walk before work in the morning, you can finish your day with another 30 minutes or more of activity in the evening when you have more time. Training sessions, in particular, should be kept short. Even a few 10- to 15-minute training sessions several times a day will add up in helping to keep your Vizsla's mind and body active. Most Vizsla owners recommend doing as much as you can in the morning before work so that your dog will be able to sleep peacefully until you return.

It's also recommended to mix up your daily activities when possible. You'll both get bored if you walk the same route around the neighborhood each and every day. A change of activity and scenery can help keep you both committed and engaged in your training journey and relationship. Plus, it's a great opportunity for socialization. For example, if you take your Vizsla hiking a few days per week, you can try new trails together or supplement your schedule with a weekly obedience class or dock diving session. As long as your Vizsla is fit and healthy, he should be up for anything you want to do.

*Photo Courtesy
of Kareen Higgins*

Photo Courtesy of Ashley Gray

Exercising Puppies

As previously mentioned, Vizsla puppies are unable to withstand long periods of physical or mental activity. Additionally, you need to be cautious about straining your dog's developing body. Many veterinarians advise against strenuous activities for dogs under about 18 months of age, as that is the age that most or all of the dog's growth plates have closed. This does not mean you shouldn't exercise your Vizsla until he reaches 18 months, but it does mean you should try not to overdo it, especially with high-impact activities such as jumping.

It's also crucial to maintain limits on your Vizsla puppy's mental activities. Puppies don't have the attention span of adult dogs, so it's important to keep training sessions short. Remember, you can repeat training sessions throughout the day, so you don't need to worry about packing a lot into each session. The recommended length of a session will depend on your puppy's age and attention span, but it's best to quit before he loses interest in what you're doing. If you regularly work your Vizsla until he's too tired to pay attention, he's going to get frustrated and will be less interested and engaged in future sessions.

The amount of physical exercise recommended for puppies is a topic of debate among dog experts. Some training programs such as Puppy Culture recommend no more than about five minutes per month of a dog's age. Under this protocol, a five-month-old Vizsla can handle up to 25 minutes of exercise per day. For some puppies, this will be enough, but others may need more. It's also not recommended to exercise the puppy for 25 minutes straight, but rather break it up into shorter sessions as you would with training. With some Vizsla puppies, you may be able to let them set their own boundaries, but particularly high-drive puppies may require you to end the session before they get too tired or hurt themselves.

Exercising Adult Dogs

A healthy adult Vizsla will be able to handle as much as several hours of strenuous exercise per day, but building fitness is as important to dogs as it is to humans. If you're working on your Vizsla's fitness, you may want to consider having your vet perform a checkup to ensure that your dog is healthy enough to begin a regular workout routine. From there, you can begin building his endurance slowly. Depending on your Vizsla's fitness level when you begin and what your goals are, it can take as much as several weeks or even months to reach your goal.

For the average pet Vizsla, it's not usually necessary to worry about performance-related injuries, but there are several areas of caution to look out for. The first is footing, as prolonged exercise on hard surfaces such as pavement can cause long-term damage to your Vizsla's joints. If you're going to take your dog jogging or play a game of fetch, it's recommended to do so on softer surfaces such as dirt or grass if possible.

Temperature is the other area of concern when it comes to exercising adult Vizslas. As discussed in an earlier chapter, Vizslas are sensitive to frigid temperatures due to their short coat. If you're going to be exercising your Vizsla in temperatures below freezing, you may want to consider having him wear a jacket or boots. If you're going to exercise your Vizsla in warm temperatures, you need to keep a close watch on him and provide him with plenty of water. If at any time he begins to pant excessively or his tongue and gums seem red rather than pink, it's time to find some shade and water.

If your Vizsla is destined to become a canine athlete and will spend his time as an active working or performance dog, fitness is a crucial aspect of making sure he can handle the exercise required by his job. You may want to consider working with a veterinarian that specializes in working or sport dogs to make sure that your Vizsla receives the care needed to keep him in top physical shape.

The Importance of Mental Exercise

The Vizsla does best with owners who are equally committed to meeting both its mental and physical demands. They need plenty of exercise, but they also need to work their minds. This means they need more mental stimulation than most breeds or they can become destructive. Vizslas also need to spend a lot of time with their owners and will take their job as devoted family protectors very seriously.

MICHEL BERNER
Mira Vizslas

Photo Courtesy
of Robyn Glynn

> *Teach the puppy something new every day. Engage in tricks train-*
> *ing. Walking and playing outside is important, but mental stimu-*
> *lation is critical with Vizslas. Set the tone with your dog in terms of*
> *teaching and learning, or he will make up his own games and they*
> *are usually not ones you like to play!*
>
> CATHY GALLAGHER
> *Sienna Pointe Vizslas*

Vizslas are an intelligent breed that not only needs to exercise their bodies on a regular basis but their minds as well. Without enough mental stimulation, a bored Vizsla may try to entertain himself by getting into trouble. As previously mentioned, mental stimulation is especially important for dogs with limited mobility, such as puppies and seniors, as well as those recovering from illnesses or injuries. For owners with mobility problems, mental exercise gives you the chance to work your dog within your physical limits. Luckily, there are many ways to exercise your Vizsla's mind without stressing his body or yours.

Mental stimulation comes from any activity that requires your Vizsla to think about his behavior and actions. The most common activity is training sessions. Training not only keeps your dog's mind and body active, but it strengthens your bond, improves his behavior, and teaches him fun new commands. Even if you don't compete with your Vizsla or need to teach him any specific commands, trick training can be a fun activity to do together.

Photo Courtesy of Ashley Lafone

As mentioned in Chapter 12, the American Kennel Club offers a Trick Dog title program that rewards dogs and handlers for learning and performing a variety of tricks. Other sports, such as scent work and barn hunt, are also a great way to engage your Vizsla's mind without being physically demanding. If sports aren't your thing, you can also use puzzle toys or snuffle mats to encourage your dog to use his mind to retrieve his favorite treats or meals.

Photo Courtesy
of Champagne Rogers

Dog Sports

> *Many people hear American Kennel Club (AKC) and think of dog shows. The AKC offers much more than that. I suggest looking into AKC activities where your dog can participate safely in fun sporting events and you can socialize with other like-minded dog owners. The AKC website offers information on Coursing, FastCAT, Agility, Canine Good Citizen, Trick Dog, Barn Hunt, Dock Diving, Scent Work, Rally, Hunting, and more. Some activities require training, while others are based more on instinct. If your dog likes to run, then maybe Coursing or FastCAT is something to look into. Loves to swim? Then try Dock Diving. Your participation can earn you a title, or do it just because your dog has fun and stays fit.*
>
> **LINDA MAUS**
> *MausHaus Vizslas*

Vizslas are a naturally athletic breed, so it's no surprise that they excel in a variety of dog sports. They are particularly talented in any sport requiring strong hunting instincts, speed, and agility. Vizslas are capable of competing in nearly any sport that is open to sporting or hunting breeds. Remember, not all Vizslas are suited for all sports, so if you have a particular activity in mind, it's important to discuss that with your breeder prior to acquiring your Vizsla. A puppy coming from a long line of field champions is far more likely to succeed in field trials than a dog without a performance pedigree. However, it's also important to remember that dogs are individuals and have their own unique preferences, so your Vizsla may enjoy a different sport than he was bred for. These versatile dogs are happy to spend any amount of time with their loved ones, so don't be afraid to try something new.

Pointing Breed Field Trials

Field trials are designed for hunting breeds to prove their natural athleticism, stamina, courage, and hunting instinct. There are two categories of field trials, one designed for retrievers and one for pointing breeds. As a pointing breed, Vizslas fall into the latter category, along with other pointing and setting breeds. Any dog of an eligible breed over the age of six months may compete.

Depending on the trial, handlers may be on foot or on horseback. As one of the oldest and most traditional field events, field trials are a fun and exciting way to embrace the Vizsla's historical purpose. Trials are also divided by stake, which provides opportunities to succeed for dogs of all ages and experience levels. At the lower levels of competition, dogs are expected to search and accurately locate and point game birds. More experienced dogs are expected to work with more speed and accuracy while also remaining steady to wing and shot, which involves the handler flushing the bird and firing a blank pistol. Once a dog earns 10 points in different stakes, he may earn the title of field champion. After earning the FC title, a dog may go on to earn the title of grand field champion (GFC).

Pointing Breed Hunt Tests

Hunt tests are unique from field trials as they are non-competitive. In the world of dog sports, trials are activities where dogs compete against each other, whereas tests are pass/fail, and dogs are not judged against any other. As with field trials, there are hunt tests for different types of hunting dogs, and Vizslas fall into the Pointing Breed category. In a Pointing Breed Hunt Test, a dog is assessed on its desire to hunt, boldness, and independence. It's also assessed on speed and the pattern in which it tracks the location of game birds. Finally, the dog is scored on its bird-finding ability, apparent trainability, and pointing. In the higher levels of competition, dogs are also scored on retrieving and honoring the game.

Other Dog Sports

66

Vizslas need a job, so hunting, agility, dock diving, or just retrieving a ball are great exercise for a Vizsla. This is also good mental stimulation, and will help ensure you don't have a couch potato!

NANCY EDMUNDS
Vizcaya Vizslas

99

Photo Courtesy of Diana Vargas

Vizslas also excel in a wide range of other dog sports, including but not limited to competitive obedience and agility. In obedience, dogs must perform specific tasks on command, including but not limited to sit, stay, heel, retrieve, and jump. There is also rally obedience, which is a faster-paced and more exciting version. Agility requires a dog and handler to navigate a course of obstacles, including jumps, tunnels, weave poles, and more. Dogs run individually but compete against others of similar size. The fastest dog with the fewest faults wins. These two sports require a high level of training, but there are classes for more novice dogs and handlers.

However, there are other sports that require less intense training to reach a competitive level. AKC offers a sport called FastCAT, which is essentially a 100-yard dash after a lure, typically resembling a plastic bag. It is a test, so dogs run one at a time and do not compete against each other. They are ranked nationally against others of the same breed but earn titles independently of their ranking. FastCAT relies on a dog's instinct to chase prey, though the owner may call the dog to encourage a faster run. If your Vizsla enjoys that, CAT, also known as CABT or Coursing Ability Test, is a longer version of FastCAT that more closely resembles lure coursing but is open to all breeds. CABT covers 600 yards and requires the dog to make turns while chasing the lure. Like FastCAT, CABT relies on the dog's instincts and does not require prior training. These two sports can be a great introduction for Vizsla and handler to the world of dog sports.

Hunting breeds also tend to excel in sports requiring the dog to search for a specific scent. Sports like barn hunt and scent work are also ideal for dogs or handlers with limited mobility. In barn hunt, dogs must search a ring filled with hay bales for a rat, which is placed safely in a PVC tube. There are different levels of competition for dogs, and dogs must find more rats with each level of difficulty. There are also empty tubes and tubes filled with rat litter to distract the dogs. In addition to finding the rats, dogs must climb on top of a bale of hay and go through a tunnel made of hay. Barn hunt is offered by the Barn Hunt Association (BHA), though titles are recognized by the AKC.

In scent work, dogs must locate a hidden scent. The scents in question are cotton swabs saturated in the essential oils of birch, anise, clove, or cypress. Depending on their experience level, dogs may search a variety of containers in different locations.

FUN FACT
Sporting Group

Vizslas are a sporting dog breed and were originally bred as companion gun dogs. Sporting dogs are excellent athletes and may enjoy hunting, agility, or other fieldwork. Some of the sporting events your Vizsla could participate in include dock diving, hunt tests, field trials, tracking, flyball, and agility.

Water-loving Vizslas may also compete in dock diving. In this sport, dogs jump off a dock into a pool of water to fetch their favorite toy. Again, there are different levels of competition to suit different levels of ability and experience. Dogs may compete for the longest distance, highest jump, or the fastest retrieve. Events are generally sponsored by either Dock Dogs or the North America Diving Dogs (NADD).

CHAPTER 15
Grooming

Coat Basics

> *Vizslas are pretty wash and wear; most stuff brushes off once dry. They generally shed their 'Vair' once a year, which a plastic curry removes well. They rarely require a bath, and the less bathing the better as it dries out their skin.*
>
> WENDY RUSSELL
> *Widdershins*

In terms of basic coat care, Vizslas are a low-maintenance breed. Their short, sleek coat requires only the occasional brushing and a bath when dirty. Most Vizslas are average shedders and typically shed consistently throughout the year rather than seasonally. Shedding may vary somewhat and will depend on several factors, including diet. To reduce shedding as much as possible, a high-quality diet and regular brushing are recommended.

Though many Vizsla owners choose to groom their dogs at home, it's also reasonable to schedule regular visits with a professional groomer. Vizslas are not large dogs but are large enough that some owners may be unwilling or unable to groom them at home. You may also consider brushing and bathing your Vizsla at home but have a professional take care of his nails. These decisions are entirely up to you, but it's important to budget accordingly. Thankfully, Vizslas are typically one of the least expensive breeds to have groomed.

Essential Grooming Tools

If you plan on grooming your Vizsla at home, or at least are considering it, you will need to invest in a few basic tools. The most important tool will be a high-quality brush. For a smooth coat, a rubber curry brush is one of the best choices, but you may also consider a boar bristle brush. Rubber curry brushes may be used on a wet or dry coat and are ideal for removing dead hair and skin cells while also stimulating blood flow in the skin. Deshedding brushes, such as the Furminator, are generally not recommended, as it's far too easy to damage the dog's coat and scratch the skin. If you would like to use this type of brush or need help with any grooming tool, consider asking your groomer for advice on safe and proper usage. Unless you're using a

*Photo Courtesy
of Tulia and Ricardo Montes*

HELPFUL TIP
How Much Do
Vizslas Shed?

Vizslas are moderate shedders and, like most other shedding breeds, will shed more during the seasonal changes in fall and spring. However, unlike other shedding breeds with longer fur, a Vizsla's shorter fur may be less noticeable on clothes and furniture. In addition, regular brushing with a soft brush can help mitigate excess fur around the house and keep your Vizsla's coat looking healthy and lustrous.

soft-bristled brush, you'll need to be cautious about brushing delicate areas such as the legs, face, and other bony areas.

If you intend to bathe your Vizsla at home, you'll need to purchase a quality shampoo. Conditioner is generally optional but may be beneficial in some cases. Both shampoos and conditioners come in a nearly endless range of formulas and scents. Remember, all Vizslas are individuals, and some may require certain types of shampoo, while others may be fine with any formula. There are gentler formulas for dogs with sensitive skin, as well as shampoos formulated for particularly dirty or smelly dogs. If your dog doesn't have any skin or coat issues, you may be able to simply choose your favorite scent.

When shopping for shampoo, it's recommended to look for a product with limited chemicals and artificial ingredients to help reduce the likelihood of irritation or a bad reaction. More natural products tend to work better for most dogs. You may also want to consider a low-sudsing shampoo. Despite the absence of bubbles, these shampoos clean just as well but typically take less time to rinse out. Conditioners are available in just as many options, but most healthy dogs don't necessarily need a conditioner. Rinse-out conditioners often lengthen the time it takes for the coat to dry, so if you need your Vizsla to dry more quickly, you might consider a leave-in spray conditioner.

Finally, you'll need to invest in a nail trimmer or grinder, whichever you'd prefer. Most dogs prefer grinders over clippers, but you may find that your Vizsla does not. If you opt for clippers, it's important to choose the scissor-style clippers over guillotine-style. The latter tends to crush the nails rather than making a clean cut. Grinders are usually the safest option as you can take thin layers off at a time to limit the risk of cutting your dog's quick. Plus, you'll be able to round the edges off, which will reduce scratches to you and your home. Grinders can be found with or without cords, so consider which will work best for you. Cords can be ungainly, but you'll need to remember to charge the batteries of a cordless model. If you need help on choosing the right tool or using the right technique, ask your groomer or vet for advice.

Bathing

> *Vizslas are naturally very clean dogs. If you need to shampoo your dog, dilute the shampoo one part shampoo to 10 parts water. Shampoos can dry out your dog's coat, and he does not need shampooing very often.*
>
> **LINDA AND JIM BUSCH**
> *Busch Vizslas*

Vizslas are one of the easiest dogs to bathe simply because their coat is so short and easy to maintain. Most of the time, excess mud and dirt simply fall away, so they don't need to be bathed too often. In fact, frequent baths can dry the skin and coat out and cause irritation. However, you also don't want to bathe your Vizsla too infrequently, as the buildup of dirt, oil, and dead hair can also cause irritation. Most groomers recommend a bath every eight to 12 weeks, but it can be done as frequently as every four weeks if your Vizsla likes to get dirty. The frequency of bathing will depend entirely on your Vizsla's lifestyle as well as your own tolerance for dirt and doggy odor.

If you are using a medicated shampoo, you'll need to check the label to see if the product needs to be applied directly to the coat. Otherwise, it's recommended to wet the dog before you apply shampoo. Wet hair helps the shampoo spread more easily, making it easier to scrub and rinse. A rubber curry is a great tool to use in the bath as it will help scrub away dirt and dead hair while also distributing the shampoo throughout the coat and ensuring it reaches the skin. Most Vizslas enjoy the bathing process, especially if you scrub in a way that provides a gentle massage.

During the bath, it's important that you avoid getting any shampoo in your Vizsla's eyes and ears. You can put cotton balls in his ears prior to the bath, but you must remember to take them out afterward. You'll also want to avoid your Vizsla's face and other delicate or bony areas if you're using a rubber curry brush to scrub. Those areas are best washed by hand.

Once you've thoroughly scrubbed your Vizsla from head to tail, you'll need to rinse the shampoo from his coat. Any residue left over will cause irritation and can lead to hot spots, so you must be thorough when rinsing. Many groomers recommend rinsing until you're sure that all the shampoo is out and then doing it once more just to be sure. If you're using conditioner,

*Photo Courtesy
of Kirsty Thomas*

you'll need to repeat this entire process with the conditioning product of your choice.

After the bath, it's time to dry. Fortunately, drying time is minimal with the Vizsla's smooth coat. Most owners opt for a quick scrub with a towel or two. This will also help to remove additional dead hair and skin cells. It's not uncommon for Vizslas to get the "zoomies" after their baths, so if you would prefer your damp dog not to run through the house rubbing on the floor and furniture, you may want to use a dryer. A handheld dryer or a high-velocity dryer like your groomer uses will remove moisture from your Vizsla's coat far faster than air drying alone. High-velocity dryers, in particular, can dry a smooth-coated dog in a matter of minutes, but they can be expensive.

Of course, you can always take your Vizsla to the groomer for his bath, where they can use their professional equipment, and you won't have to worry about any cleanup afterward.

Brushing

Even though Vizslas have a "wash and wear" coat, it does still require brushing, especially if you aren't a fan of having dog hair on your clothes and furniture. By brushing your dog a few times per week, you'll not only keep his skin and coat healthy, but you'll also minimize his shedding.

As mentioned in previous sections, rubber curry brushes are ideal for smooth-coated breeds such as the Vizsla. However, the tool is only effective if the person using it knows what he or she is doing. You must be sure to use enough pressure that the brush effectively removes dirt and dead hair—but not enough to cause discomfort. You'll also need to be careful around your Vizsla's private area, legs, face, and tail, as these areas can be sensitive and may require less pressure. You can also use a soft-bristled brush on more delicate areas if you'd like. If you're struggling to develop the right technique or you aren't sure about your tools, ask your groomer to demonstrate for you the next time you make an appointment.

Cleaning Eyes and Ears

Most Vizslas experience few problems with their eyes and ears, but that doesn't mean you should overlook their care. Part of the grooming process should include checking over every inch of your dog to make sure there are no problems. This way, any potential infections or irritation can be addressed right away. It's generally recommended to clean your Vizsla's ears after baths and swimming sessions to remove any trapped moisture that could lead to an ear infection.

If your Vizsla is experiencing any problems with his ears, you may notice him scratching at one or both ears or rubbing his head on the floor. Inside the ear, you may see redness or swelling, and an unpleasant odor may be present. If your Vizsla is experiencing any of these symptoms, you'll need to take him to the vet as ear infections cannot be treated at home, especially if you aren't sure whether it's a yeast or bacterial infection.

To properly clean your Vizsla's ears, you need to purchase an appropri-ate ear cleaner. Some ear cleaners contain alcohol, so it's important to read the label before you buy. Alcohol-based cleaners are great for drying out ears after baths and swimming since they evaporate so quickly, but they can be irritating to sensitive or infected ears. Non-alcohol ear cleaners tend to be gentler but do not evaporate as quickly. You'll also need cotton balls rather than swabs. Cotton swabs may accidentally be inserted too far into the ear, causing pain and damage, but cotton balls used with your fingers are generally harmless.

Thoroughly wet the cotton with cleaner and squeeze out any excess product. Gently insert the cotton ball into the ear and clean with gentle circular motions. You may also wipe the inside of the ear canal if a discharge is present. If your Vizsla has an ear infection, he may be sensitive about any handling of his ears, so you'll need to be careful not to hurt him. After you've cleaned his ears, you can go over the area with a dry cotton ball to absorb the excess cleaner. Otherwise, your Vizsla may shake it out all over your house.

Vizslas don't usually experience tear staining, but they can occasionally have a bit of crusty discharge in the corners of their eyes. This can be removed with a soft cloth. You may also use a damp cloth or eye wipes if you'd like. As you clean the area around your Vizsla's eyes, be sure not to accidentally scratch or poke his eye. If your dog's eyes ever seem excessively watery or there is unusual discharge, you need to take him to the vet as soon as possible so that any infection or other medical problem can be addressed.

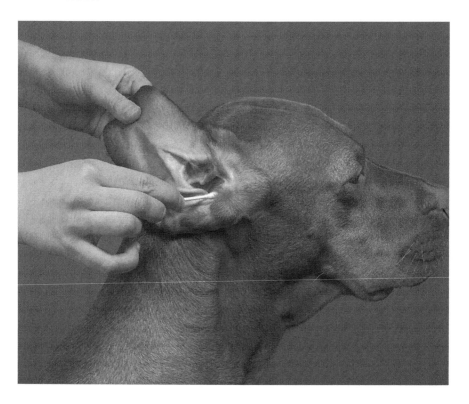

Trimming Nails

> 66
>
> *As a puppy, hold your Vizsla in a cradled position so he learns to be still while you are touching his feet and trimming his nails. This will help him understand that he must allow his feet to be touched and his nails to be trimmed as he gets older.*
>
> RHONDA J CHESLEY
> *Midwest Dream*
>
> 99

Nail trimming needs to be done on a regular basis; otherwise, your Vizsla's long nails will begin to affect his gait and musculoskeletal structure. These changes can be particularly damaging when the dog in question is young and still developing, though discomfort can occur at any age. Nails grow at different rates, and your Vizsla's lifestyle and activity level will affect how often you need to trim his nails. If he walks on pavement often, that may wear his nails down naturally, and he may need less frequent trims. But if he spends most of his time on softer surfaces, his nails may need to be trimmed more often. Some owners choose to trim their Vizsla's nails as often as every week, while others may prefer a monthly schedule. As long as they aren't left long enough to affect your dog's movement, you may choose how often you trim his nails.

If you're planning on trimming your Vizsla's nails yourself, you'll need to first locate the quick, which is the nails' blood supply. If trimmed too short, the quick will bleed, and your dog will experience pain. On light-colored nails, you should be able to see the quick from the side, but it's going to be more difficult if your Vizsla has dark nails. It's recommended to take thin layers off the nail, regardless of color, to avoid "quicking" your dog. As you take each layer off with your clippers or grinder, look for a darker circle at the center of the nail. Once you locate that spot, stop trimming, as that is the end of the quick. Further trimming will result in pain and bleeding. However, even professional groomers quick a dog on occasion, so you may consider having styptic powder or gel on hand to stop the bleeding if you accidentally trim too far. Repeat this process for each nail, and don't forget the dewclaws if your Vizsla has them.

Nail trimming isn't difficult, but it can take practice to get the handling and trimming techniques down. It's understandable if you'd prefer not to do this yourself. It can be especially challenging for the average Vizsla owner if the dog is difficult to handle during the process. Fortunately, most vets and groomers will do it for a relatively low price, often under $20. Though the procedure takes only a few minutes, some groomers and vets will require you to have an appointment, while others may allow walk-ins. Always call beforehand to verify, and don't forget to tip your groomer!

I begin using a Dremel to file nails on puppies at the age of one month. I file puppy nails every three days thereafter because nails grow so fast and it is part of their training. Teaching your dog to accept being restricted by holding his paw, letting him hear the sound of the Dremel, and getting into a routine will make this process easier for both of you in the long run. Make it a positive experience by gently filing the nails and giving a treat reward after each paw.

LINDA MAUS
MausHaus Vizslas

Brushing Your Dog's Teeth

Dental care is an important part of keeping your Vizsla happy and healthy, but at-home teeth brushing can help extend the amount of time between professional cleanings. If you doubt the importance of brushing your Vizsla's teeth, consider how your own teeth might look if you only relied on your dentist cleaning them once or twice per year. Regular brushing will also help you to monitor your dog's dental health so that you can spot and address any problems as soon as possible. Depending on what you feed your Vizsla, plaque and tartar can develop quickly, and periodontal disease may develop. Without regular dental care, the bacteria present in plaque and tartar can enter the bloodstream and spread throughout your dog's body. Left unchecked, serious illness and tooth loss can occur.

In order to properly brush your Vizsla's teeth, you'll need to use the correct tools. There are many styles of toothbrushes designed for dogs, but most owners choose the ones that resemble human toothbrushes or those that slip over the finger. Neither style is superior to the other, so it's a matter of personal preference. Some owners also choose to use children's toothbrushes, as they are easier to find than dog-specific toothbrushes. When

Photo Courtesy of Madison Rice

it comes to toothpaste, never use products designed for humans. Human toothpaste contains ingredients that are unsafe for dogs, including xylitol, which can be deadly to dogs. Instead, look for a toothpaste formulated for dogs or make a paste out of baking soda and water.

If you've never brushed your Vizsla's teeth before, you'll need to start slowly to ensure you make it a positive experience for him. If your doggie toothpaste is flavored, consider putting a bit on your finger for him to lick off. You can then put some on the toothbrush for him to lick off before progressing to actually brushing his teeth. You may not be able to brush all of his teeth during the first session, but go slow and give him plenty of praise and affection for behaving. Brush gently at first, even if it doesn't seem to be removing any tartar. You can increase pressure as the dog gets used to it, but you want to make it a pleasant experience for him at first.

No matter how often you brush your Vizsla's teeth at home, you'll still need to take him to the vet for professional cleanings on occasion. Depending on your dog's health, your vet may recommend yearly or twice-yearly checkups. It's worth noting that professional teeth cleanings are done under anesthesia, but the procedure is incredibly safe. However, if you have any questions or concerns about anesthesia or the procedure itself, be sure to ask your vet.

CHAPTER 16
Basic Health Care

Even the healthiest Vizsla will visit the vet on a regular basis throughout his life. Some dogs may only need a yearly checkup, while others may need to see the vet twice per year or more. Though it may seem silly to take your dog to the vet when he's healthy, it's a crucial part of keeping him in top health. Many health issues can progress quickly, so it's important to catch them in the early stages and begin treatment as soon as possible.

Photo Courtesy of Melissa and Drew Wall

It's your responsibility to monitor your Vizsla's health at home, but you will not be able to test him for internal parasites, such as intestinal worms and heartworms. Seeing your dog every day can also make it difficult for you to notice gradual changes, whereas your vet will be able to do so by comparing his or her notes from your last visit. The exact frequency at which your Vizsla will need checkups will depend on many factors, so it's best to ask your vet for advice.

Allergies

Though Vizslas are generally a healthy breed, it's not uncommon for them to be diagnosed with allergies. Allergies typically appear in dogs over six months of age, but most are not diagnosed until one or two years. It is unknown why some dogs develop allergies while others do not, and some experts believe there may be a genetic cause, though this has yet to be proven. A dog's immune system may react to any allergen in the environment, but the most common are food, plants, insects, and other species of animals.

The exact symptoms of allergies will depend heavily on the allergen and the way it enters the body. Generalized or localized itching, coughing, sneezing, and watery eyes are common. Dogs with food allergies may experience vomiting or diarrhea, along with more generalized itching. Yeast infections in the ears and paws are also common. Dogs that are allergic to specific plants, insects, or other animals may experience itching, swelling, redness, and hives near where they were exposed to the allergen. Allergens that enter through the respiratory system may cause symptoms such as sneezing, coughing, wheezing, or difficulty breathing.

Unfortunately, allergies are not an easy diagnosis. Treatment is generally most effective when the veterinary team knows what the dog is allergic to, but narrowing it down is not an easy task. Testing tends to be inaccurate in many cases, and it can take weeks or even months to determine a potential cause for

HELPFUL TIP
Recognizing Hypothyroidism

Vizslas can be prone to developing hypothyroidism, a treatable condition diagnosed by a blood test. Symptoms of hypothyroidism in dogs include unexplained weight gain, lethargy, excessive shedding and balding, and increased ear infections. Hypothyroidism isn't a curable disease but is treatable through hormone replacement. Untreated hypothyroidism will lead to worsening conditions and possibly serious complications.

allergies. Consider how many ingredients are in your Vizsla's food and how many plants, insects, and animals he may interact with on any given day.

Once the allergen is known, treatment can be simple, but sometimes limiting the dog's exposure to the allergen is not possible. In some cases, the symptoms may be difficult to control with injectable or oral antihistamines. Some dogs may be soothed with medicated shampoos, conditioners, or ointments, but topical treatments are rarely a permanent solution to the problem. Dogs that are allergic to certain ingredients in their food may need to be fed specific diets, including hypoallergenic diets, as discussed earlier in this book. Allergies are typically not life-threatening but can cause serious discomfort. If you believe your Vizsla may have allergies, you should consult your veterinarian as soon as possible.

Photo Courtesy of Cynthia Hughes

Fleas and Ticks

The more time a Vizsla spends outside, the more likely he is to pick up fleas and ticks from the environment. External parasites can carry a range of dangerous diseases, some of which are zoonotic, so prevention is key. Fleas can carry tapeworms and Bartonellosis and can cause flea allergy dermatitis and anemia. Different species of ticks carry different diseases, including but not limited to Lyme disease, babesiosis, and ehrlichiosis. Fortunately, there are many products on the market formulated for flea and tick prevention. However, some products will cover some species of parasite but not others, so it's important to ask your vet which product is best in your location. You may also need to apply it part of the year or year-round, depending on your area and climate. It's important to note that if you board your Vizsla or take him to doggie daycare, you may be required to apply flea and tick preventative before dropping him off.

Most experts recommend against flea and tick collars, as many contain an ingredient called tetrachlorvinphos. This chemical is considered carcinogenic by the Environmental Protection Agency and can cause serious reactions, including hair loss, irritation, diarrhea, and vomiting. Some pets may also experience more severe reactions such as seizures and death. If you have cats in your home, you will need to avoid tetrachlorvinphos, as cats tend to be more sensitive and prone to more serious reactions.

Internal Parasites

Though Vizslas of all ages may contract internal parasites, it's especially common with puppies. Puppies can easily pick up parasites from their mother or their environment since they tend to explore with their mouths. Most parasites are contracted when contaminated water, food, soil, or feces is consumed by the dog. Though most internal parasites are easy to treat, they can cause serious health problems, and many can be transferred to humans.

The most common internal parasites are intestinal parasites such as roundworms, tapeworms, whipworms, and hookworms. The specific parasites your Vizsla is at risk of contracting will depend on where you live. Protozoa such as giardia and coccidia are also common.

One of the most dangerous internal parasites is the heartworm. As the name suggests, heartworms can be found in the heart and bloodstream and are transmitted by mosquitos. Heartworms are more serious than most internal parasites as they can cause permanent damage to the heart and

Photo Courtesy
of Zoraida Abresch

other vital organs and can be fatal if left untreated. Treatment generally takes several months, during which the dog must stay as inactive as possible. Rest is required because as the worms die off in the bloodstream, strenuous activity can cause them to pile up and block vital arteries. Heartworm is preventable with a monthly chewable tablet that can be prescribed by your veterinarian.

Though some dogs will exhibit symptoms of internal parasites, many will not, so regular testing is crucial. Possible symptoms may include sudden weight loss, coughing, lethargy, vomiting, and diarrhea. Some dogs may also have a distended stomach and an otherwise malnourished appearance. Anemia is also common with heavy parasite loads.

To test for intestinal parasites, your vet will collect a fecal sample, which will be examined under a microscope to see the eggs, larvae, and adults of whatever parasite may be present. Treatment varies according to the specific parasite present but may include injectable or oral medications. Heartworm tests require a small blood sample, which is mixed with a chemical solution and poured into a disposable testing device. After a few minutes, the results will be available. Heartworm treatment will vary by case but be prepared for several months of regular treatment and lifestyle management for your dog.

177

Vaccinations

The specific vaccines your Vizsla will require will depend on his age, lifestyle, and the area in which you live. Some vaccines, such as those that protect against rabies, distemper, and parvovirus, will be given no matter where you live and may even be required by law. These are often referred to as core vaccines. Others, known as non-core vaccines, may not be necessary for your dog, but it's always best to ask your veterinarian about which ones are appropriate for your Vizsla.

Core vaccines protect your Vizsla against the most common diseases that he may encounter. Some viruses, such as rabies, are zoonotic, meaning they can be transferred to humans. This is why rabies vaccines are usually required by law in countries where the rabies virus is present. Additionally, the rabies vaccine must be administered by a licensed veterinarian and is not one that you can do at home. The minimum age for rabies vaccination is 16 weeks, though most dogs will require a booster at around one year of age. After that, rabies vaccines may be given every one to three years, depending on local regulations.

The other common core vaccine is known as DHPP. It protects against parvovirus, distemper, parainfluenza, hepatitis, and adenovirus cough. Most puppies receive this vaccine at regular intervals, usually at six, twelve, and sixteen weeks of age. As adults, it's given every one to three years depending on local regulations as well as your vet's recommendation. Some DHPP vaccines may also protect against canine coronavirus and/or leptospirosis.

Your veterinarian may also recommend a Bordetella vaccine, which is a non-core vaccine that protects against kennel cough. Though generally not deadly, kennel cough is highly contagious and can require prolonged treatment. If you frequently take your Vizsla to doggie daycare, a boarding facility, or the groomer, proof of this vaccination may be required prior to drop-off. Other non-core vaccines may protect against leptospirosis, Lyme disease, and rattlesnake venom. It's important to note that while core vaccines protect for upwards of a year, most non-core vaccines may provide as little as six months of protection, so they'll need to be administered more frequently.

Allergic reactions to vaccines are incredibly rare but not impossible. To minimize the potential for reactions, many owners choose to have their vet administer one vaccine at a time. For example, if your Vizsla is due for DHPP and rabies, you may want to administer DHPP at the initial appointment and rabies at another appointment a few weeks later. If your Vizsla is sensitive to vaccines, this will not eliminate the possibility of a reaction, but it will minimize it as much as possible. Common allergic reactions include lethargy, vomiting, hives, and swelling of the face or paws. Some dogs may also experience swelling or pain at the injection site. More severe reactions can include difficulty breathing and seizures. If you know your Vizsla has a history of allergic reactions, or you don't yet know him well enough to rule it out, consider staying near the vet clinic for 20 to 30 minutes after the injection so that you can seek medical help quickly if necessary.

Titer testing is another option for Vizslas that are sensitive for vaccines or owners who want to avoid over-vaccinating their dog. In some areas, it is a legal alternative to core vaccines. Titer testing involves the collection of a blood sample, which is then submitted to a veterinary lab to measure the antibody levels. If the levels are adequate, the dog may skip vaccination at that time. Titer testing varies in cost and may be expensive in some areas, but the extra cost is worth minimizing the risk to sensitive Vizslas.

Spaying and Neutering

If you purchased your Vizsla from a shelter or rescue organization, it's likely that he or she has already been spayed or neutered, so you don't need to worry about making choices about your dog's reproductive health. However, if you've purchased a puppy or unaltered adult, you'll need to decide whether to spay or neuter and when you want to have it done.

Photo Courtesy
of Ashley Gray

Neutering typically refers to the removal of the testicles of male dogs, but in some cases may refer to females too. Spaying is the more common term to refer to the removal of the ovaries and uterus of a female dog. For most pet owners, the choice to spay or neuter is obvious, as they do not want the responsibility of maintaining their dog's reproductive health and preventing unwanted pregnancies. However, if your Vizsla is a show dog, you may need to keep him intact in order to compete, though some organizations offer a class for altered dogs. If you plan on competing in sports, your dog will still be able to compete regardless of whether he's been altered.

179

In recent years, the previously recommended guidelines regarding spaying and neutering have been a topic of debate. Some countries, such as Norway, legally prohibit sterilization unless it's done for specific medical reasons. Many American vets recommend spaying or neutering around the age of six months because the average dog owner is not able to manage an unaltered dog and prevent accidental breeding. However, recent research has shown that there are drawbacks to pediatric spaying and neutering. It's important to note that these procedures may not be appropriate for every dog.

Though surgical sterilization can prevent the development of testicular or ovarian cancer, research has shown that some dogs may experience an increase in aggression or behavioral problems. Research has also shown that dogs that have been sterilized at a young age are at a higher risk of developing orthopedic disorders such as hip dysplasia and cruciate ligament rupture. The reproductive organs are responsible for the production of certain growth hormones, so once they are removed, the bones grow differently than if the dog remained unaltered. To reduce the risk of behavioral or orthopedic issues, some vets are now recommending waiting until dogs are fully grown, at around 18 to 24 months of age, before spaying or neutering.

An increasing number of veterinarians are also offering surgical alternatives that eliminate the risk of accidental pregnancy while allowing the dog to keep his or her hormones intact. A vasectomy is a minimally invasive procedure that leaves the dog's testicles intact but transects the spermatic cord so that the dog is rendered infertile. Female dogs may undergo an ovary-sparing spay (OSS) to remove the uterus and cervix but leave the ovaries intact to continue hormone production.

The decision to spay or neuter your Vizsla and at what age is not a decision to be taken lightly. However, it's best to discuss your concerns with your veterinarian, who will be able to evaluate your dog's overall health and lifestyle to determine the right course of action. Remember, all surgical procedures have their own unique risks and benefits, so be sure to keep an open mind during your discussion with your vet.

Holistic Alternatives

If you prefer a more holistic approach to your own health care, you may want to consider doing the same for your Vizsla. Depending on where you're located, you may have a holistic veterinary clinic nearby. If you are not familiar with the concept of holistic care, it's important to understand that it's not just alternative treatments such as acupuncture and herbal supplements but a combination of conventional and alternative treatments. Holistic veterinarians attend the same universities as traditional vets and offer many of the same treatments. They simply supplement their treatment plans with alternatives such as nutritional therapy, massage, and chiropractic care.

Holistic medicine addresses problems by treating the body as a whole rather than just treating the site of the specific problem. For example, at a conventional clinic, a dog with skin problems may be given oral or topical medication to remedy his symptoms. A holistic vet will instead look at

Photo Courtesy of Debbie Day

ways to improve the dog's overall health by addressing his diet and lifestyle, as well as providing topical or oral medications when needed. This alternative approach can be especially helpful for dogs suffering from chronic health problems.

If you'd like to find a holistic veterinarian in your area, the American Holistic Veterinary Medical Association's website has a list of holistic vets in the US and Canada. The list can be searched by species and specialty, so you'll be able to track down the perfect vet for your Vizsla.

Pet Insurance

Given the rising cost of veterinary care in the United States, it's only natural for owners to explore options that might mitigate the cost of caring for their beloved Vizslas. In recent years, many companies have begun offering pet insurance policies with a range of premium prices and coverage levels. Some policies may cover only emergencies, while others may also cover preventative care. Not all policies are the same, so it's important to do your research if this is something you'd like to consider. As with human insurance policies, senior dogs or dogs with preexisting health conditions may cost more to insure or may be denied coverage.

Some owners swear by pet insurance as it has helped to cover the cost of expensive emergency care for their Vizsla, while others may pay a monthly premium for years without ever having to need it. As part of your research, you'll need to decide whether the benefits of the plan are worth the monthly cost. If your Vizsla is a healthy adult that is not prone to injury, you may be paying for a policy you don't need. Some owners choose to set aside a certain amount of money each month to save for an emergency rather than giving that money to an insurance company. Pet insurance isn't right for every owner, so be sure to thoroughly research your options before committing to a decision.

CHAPTER 17
The Aging Vizsla

> Dogs age just like people. The first outward sign of aging is white fur. We call them Sugar Vizslas when they turn white. Other changes begin that you may not notice right away. They may need to nap more, have less interest in everyday activities or toys, be easily startled, or lack patience with other dogs and children. Their vision and hearing will decline. Some become incontinent, can't find their beds, or get lost in their own homes. They still crave human attention. At this stage, your dog may not be able to go for that long walk like he used to, but take him for a shorter walk. It's about being together and keeping some experiences dear while other senses and activities are fleeting. If your dog becomes incontinent or loses his vision, refer back to the good old puppy days. Give him a safe gated space and remove any items that may cause him harm. Life is temporary for all of us. Your dog has given you so much joy during his lifetime, and he asks for nothing in return. The most helpful thing you can do is to show him patience, kindness, and be there for him during this transition.
>
> **LINDA MAUS**
> *MausHaus Vizslas*

Basics of Senior Dog Care

Vizslas are typically considered to be seniors at around seven years of age. Not all dogs age at the same rate, so some Vizslas may begin to act like seniors much earlier or later. Additionally, the signs of aging will vary as well. Some dogs may begin getting tired more quickly during physical activity but remain the same otherwise, while others may struggle with their hearing or vision. Some Vizslas will gray around their face and muzzle, while others may age without a single gray hair.

It's also possible that the signs of aging may appear so slowly that you may not recognize them right away. Some common signs of aging include sleeping more during the day, struggling to get up in the morning, or not having the endurance they once had. For senior dogs that begin losing their sight or hearing, you'll need to be careful not to startle them. Changes in metabolism may also cause your Vizsla to gain or lose weight. Many older dogs also begin losing control over their bladder or bowels, so they may not be able to go as long between bathroom breaks. One of the most heart-breaking signs of aging is cognitive dysfunction or dementia, which typically presents as temporary confusion or changes in behavior. As you begin to notice these changes in your Vizsla, you'll need to begin adjusting your home and care to accommodate his needs.

Photo Courtesy
of Kristen and Vince Colapietro

Veterinary Care for Senior Dogs

> *Hopefully, one has gotten their Vizsla from a breeder that breeds for structure. Then, it is up to the home to keep this structure healthy (starting with appropriate activity for a puppy), and then to keep the Vizsla active throughout the senior years. Chiropractic checkups and physical therapy contribute to keep the healthy structure. Short nails help to keep the feet healthy and support good posture. Always be careful about repetitive activities with fast stops and turns, such as fetch, and be wary of activities that cause torque and stress on the spine (like Frisbee). Finally, don't allow jumping into an SUV or off high beds.*
>
> JUDY HETKOWSKI
> *Boulder Vizslas*

Most veterinarians recommend more frequent checkups for senior dogs, sometimes as often as every six months or more, depending on your Vizsla's health. Many age-related conditions progress quickly, so it's important to keep a close eye on any developing issues. Some vets recommend twice yearly bloodwork as an additional level of monitoring to make sure your Vizsla enters his golden years in the best shape possible. It's not uncommon for a dog's dental health to decline as he ages, so your senior Vizsla may also require more frequent dental cleanings than he did in his youth.

One benefit of more frequent checkups is the opportunity to ask your vet about any concerns you may have about your aging Vizsla. Owners that haven't cared for older dogs before may need help navigating the challenges of senior care. There may also be nutritional supplements or medications to help maintain your senior's quality of life. Remember, any sudden changes in weight or behavior can be a sign of a serious health problem, so be sure to consult your veterinarian as soon as possible.

Nutritional Changes

Most senior Vizslas require some change to their diet to accommodate their changing metabolism. The specific changes needed will be determined by your Vizsla's overall health and physical fitness. An especially

185

Photo Courtesy
of Christie Carlson

active working or sport Vizsla that once required a tremendous amount of food each day may need a significant reduction in daily calories to maintain a healthy weight. Excess weight is particularly unhealthy for seniors as it increases the stress on weakening and arthritic joints. Some seniors may also benefit from a change of food or the addition of nutritional supplements.

If your senior Vizsla begins losing weight or his appetite just isn't what it used to be, you may want to consider changing his diet or adding tasty toppers to his meals. Some seniors may have dental issues that require a softer food, while others just need something more appetizing. It's import-ant to note that if your Vizsla experiences any significant changes in weight, it's best to have your veterinarian check over him before changing his diet, as the changes may be related to a health issue rather than just his appetite.

If your Vizsla does develop a health problem as he ages, he may also require a special diet. Prescription diets, such as those formulated for heart or kidney problems, are commonly prescribed to older dogs. Vizslas that suffer from limited mobility may benefit from food or supplements with glucosamine, chondroitin, MSM, or green-lipped mussel in them. Additional fiber, probiotics, or digestive enzymes can benefit older dogs with diges-tive issues. Again, before you begin adding supplements or changing your aging Vizsla's diet, consult your veterinarian to rule out any serious health problems.

Exercising the Senior Dog

> *Keep your dog young by giving him a job doing easy performance activities (barn hunt, obedience, rally, scent work). Just because he is a senior dog doesn't mean he wants to sit on the couch all day.*
>
> JANET LAMAN
> *Valhalla Vizslas*

As your Vizsla begins to slow down in his old age, you'll need to adjust his exercise routine accordingly. Most senior dogs will require a reduction in the duration and intensity of their physical activities as their bodies begin to change. Your Vizsla will have less stamina, and he may begin to appear less enthusiastic about his favorite activities. Most older Vizslas begin to enjoy more time on the sofa or their favorite dog bed. However, it's important to maintain some form of physical activity with your senior dog, even if it's just a few minutes at a time. You might also consider introducing activities with less impact, such as swimming.

In addition to reducing your Vizsla's physical exercise, you may want to consider introducing more mentally challenging activities into his daily schedule. If he's no longer able to go for long walks, you can supplement his shorter walk with a puzzle toy or scent work session. More mental exercise will keep your senior Vizsla happy and fulfilled, even if he's not able to do the physically demanding activities he once enjoyed.

You may also want to consider changing the environment in which you exercise your Vizsla. Exercising on hard surfaces, such as pavement, can be jarring on arthritic joints, so consider walking your dog somewhere softer, such as a grassy park or dirt trail if possible. You may also want to avoid difficult terrain as well as stairs to avoid any potential injuries. New scenery will also keep your Vizsla interested in the activity and expose him to new sights and smells.

HELPFUL TIP
Life Expectancy

Vizslas live an average of 12 to 15 years, but the oldest Vizsla is rumored to have lived an impressive 21 years! The VCA conducted a health survey in 2008, which determined that out of 400 deceased Vizslas, the mean life span was about 9.15 years.

Household Changes

In order to keep your senior Vizsla happy, healthy, and injury-free, you may need to make some changes around your home. Older dogs typically don't have the strength they had in their youth, so they may struggle to keep their footing on slick or uneven surfaces. Flooring such as hardwood or tile can become a hazard to older dogs, so you may want to invest in a few rugs to place in key areas to help your dog stay upright. You can also have him wear grippy socks in the house, though it's not recommended to leave them on if he's left unsupervised.

Pressure-mounted baby gates are also a great way to limit your Vizsla's access to dangerous areas of the home, such as stairs, without making permanent changes to your home. If your Vizsla spends a lot of time on the furniture, you may consider

Photo Courtesy of Sharon Reinert

placing steps or ramps to make it easier for him or provide him with lower alternatives. If you have long flights of stairs that cannot be avoided, there are also special harnesses to help owners aid their dogs in navigating these challenging obstacles without injury.

If your aging Vizsla suffers from cognitive dysfunction, you'll need to be especially careful about your home environment. Stairs, open doors, and pools can be particularly dangerous to a confused older dog. Even if he previously knew how to get out of certain areas of the home or yard, he may not be able to do so in a state of confusion. You will need to limit his access to areas of your home or yard for his own safety, especially during any periods where he is not supervised. Though some of these home alterations may seem extreme, it's far better than the potential tragedy that could occur otherwise.

Preparing to Say Goodbye

> "
>
> *I would say that putting a dog down because of its potty messes is never an option. But, when your dog starts to fail and is in pain and you can see it in your dog, you might consider options. Things to consider would be when your dog no longer can stand on its feet, especially to get up to get outside, when it suffers pain and cries, and when it can't function eating. Your vet will help you with this. While we don't want to lose our dogs too soon, we also don't want them to suffer old, painful age.*
>
> **STEPHEN J SHLYEN**
> *Rheingold Vizslas*
>
> "

As painful and heart-wrenching as it can be to say goodbye to our beloved pets, the time will come for you to do so with your Vizsla. For some, this time may come unexpectedly soon, while others may have more time to prepare. No matter what happens, always prioritize your Vizsla's quality of life and appreciate every moment you have with him. There may come a time where you'll need to make the heartbreaking decision to send him over the Rainbow Bridge.

Humane euthanasia is a painless procedure that ensures that your Vizsla does not suffer in his last few moments on this earth. A licensed veterinarian will inject your Vizsla with a lethal overdose of sodium pentobarbital, which will stop his heart. In most cases, your dog will be sedated prior to this final injection to further relax him, especially if he's nervous or in pain. Once the sodium pentobarbital enters the bloodstream, it takes just seconds for the heart to stop.

This procedure can be performed in your home or in your vet's office. Though it can be difficult to think about your last moments with your beloved Vizsla, it's important to plan ahead so that you don't have to make important decisions amid your grief and pain. If you have the opportunity, consider talking to your vet about end-of-life services. Not all clinics offer in-home euthanasia, but some do. No matter where it happens, the most important thing is that you're with your best friend in his final moments.

You'll also need to decide what you want to do with your Vizsla's remains. Your veterinarian will have a few different options available, including cremation. If cremation is your choice, you may have the remains taken care of, or you may have them returned to you. Again, if you have the opportunity to explore your options ahead of time, you may be able to give your vet specific instructions to follow so that when the time comes, you can focus on your goodbyes rather than the arrangements.

Quality of Life

It can be difficult for anyone, even professionals, to determine the right time to say goodbye to a pet. However, it's often said that it's better to do it a week too early than a day too late. This simply means that it's better to say goodbye when your Vizsla is still happy and enjoying himself rather than after a period of suffering. Fortunately, the Quality-of-Life Scale, created by Alice Villalobos, helps caregivers to decide whether to continue a dog's end-of-life care or say goodbye. The factors of a dog's life that should be considered when evaluating quality of life are hurt, hunger, hydration, hygiene, happiness, and mobility. Each factor can be scored on a scale of 1 to 10 points. A score of over 35 represents a quality of life that is acceptable enough to continue care. Any score below 35 represents a poor quality of life, and humane euthanasia should be considered.

The first factor, hurt, considers whether a pet's pain is under control and he is able to breathe properly. If the dog cannot breathe and there is no way to improve the situation, euthanasia needs to be considered. If an animal's pain is manageable and oxygen supplementation can get them through this episode, continued care is recommended.

The second factor, hunger, covers a dog's appetite and ability to eat. If the dog is able to eat enough nutritious food to maintain his weight, his quality of life is not suffering. Temporary hand-feeding or a feeding tube is acceptable, but the hope is that the dog will return to eating on his own. If the dog is unable to eat enough food for the foreseeable future, euthanasia should be discussed. The same goes for hydration. If the dog requires temporary fluids to stay hydrated, that's fine, but if the dog

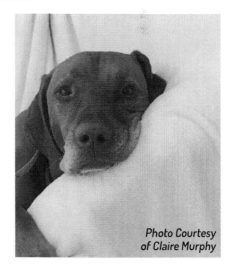

Photo Courtesy of Claire Murphy

is constantly dehydrated and unable to drink on his own, his quality of life is not ideal.

An animal's hygiene should always be considered when discussing quality of life. If you are able to keep your Vizsla clean, well-groomed, and free from parasites, that is an ideal quality of life. However, if the dog eliminates on himself regularly and you are unable to manage his hygiene, this will represent a poor score in this category.

Happiness can be a difficult factor to evaluate, but you need to consider how much joy and interest your Vizsla has in day-to-day activities. Is he responsive to his favorite people, toys, or treats, or does he seem depressed, anxious, or afraid? The more joy your dog expresses daily, the higher the score.

The final factor to consider in quality of life is mobility. A dog that stumbles, has seizures, requires assistance to get up or move will receive a poor score in this category. However, if the dog's mobility can be improved with amputation or a doggie wheelchair, and you are able to provide a solution, a higher score is recommended. For owners with limited mobility themselves, it can be difficult to care for a dog with limited mobility, so this should be considered during evaluation.

Additionally, the number of good days compared to bad days should be considered when scoring a dog's quality of life. If the number of days where the dog seems ill, frustrated, in pain, or otherwise suffering outnumber the days of happiness, his quality of life may be too compromised to continue care. Ideally, euthanasia should be considered before the bad days outnumber the good to allow the dog to pass peacefully and painlessly. Every pet owner understands how difficult it is to make this decision, but if you feel that your Vizsla's quality of life isn't what it once was, consider discussing the topic with your veterinarian.

Grief and Healing

Anyone who has ever been blessed with the love of an animal understands the grief and pain of losing a cherished pet. The grieving period after saying goodbye to your Vizsla will be difficult, but it's important to understand that you are not alone. Do not let yourself get wrapped up in your doubts and regrets. You did the best you could for your Vizsla, and he loved you unconditionally. During this difficult time, you might consider reaching out to friends and family for comfort. If they knew your Vizsla well, you can remember all the good memories you had together. If you have other pets, remember to give them extra affection and appreciate every moment you have with them.

For some grieving owners, memorializing their Vizslas can help navigate painful emotions. Artists and companies around the world offer personalized memorials. You may find jewelry, garden décor items, ceramic tiles, or statues that can be personalized as you see fit. You may also want to consider making a donation in your Vizsla's name, such as to a breed rescue group or local shelter. Planting trees or flowers, or volunteering in your community, may also help you with your grief while also helping or bringing joy to others.

No matter what you're feeling during this difficult time, understand that your feelings are normal. Everyone has a different experience with grief, and it's common for some people to struggle more than others. If you are having a particularly difficult time with your grief, consider contacting a grief counselor. A mental health professional will be able to guide you through your pain and give you new coping skills to deal with your loss and process your feelings. No matter how you choose to grieve, know that time heals all wounds. It may not feel like it during the first few weeks or months, but the pain will eventually lessen. As you grieve, don't forget to cherish the memories you made with your beloved Vizsla, and remember that he loved you every bit as much as you loved him.

Made in United States
Orlando, FL
23 January 2024

42812098R00111